Robert Ironside

Wm Bowie

A F Hall

John Willocks

John Easton

Charles Brodie

Letitia M. P. Whiteside

A.H. Ross

George H Pennian

J H Curie

J Jones

Jas Inglis

F F Scott

H Goldie

John Easton

Thos D. F. Scott

D. F. MacDonald

Hector Mac Iver

Jno B. Innes

D Mitchell

W Monkett

A. R. Graham

John Cunningham

Alexander Aitken

William Cochrane

James S Preston

W. Abyatherow

R. A. Trotter

Nigel McHase

G.J. Thornton.

Douglas. Telford.

Iain Bell

Robert Forrester.

A. Scott Lindsay

Robin M. Murray.

Ian Nixon

Michael Fowler

John. Whitney

William Magill

Brian Park

RWJ Keith

Norman Thomas.

Ian Forsyth.

Thomas Buick

Peter R. Lewis

Colin Brown

THE ROYAL HIGH SCHOOL

TO THOSE WHO SERVED
1914-1918
1939-1945

William C. G. Ross.

THE
ROYAL HIGH SCHOOL

BY

WILLIAM C. A. ROSS, M.A.

LATE DEPUTY RECTOR AND HISTORY MASTER

OLIVER AND BOYD

EDINBURGH: TWEEDDALE COURT
LONDON: 98 GREAT RUSSELL ST., W.C.

First Published 1934
Second Edition 1949

PRINTED FOR THE PUBLISHERS BY
ROBERT CUNNINGHAM AND SONS LTD., ALVA

PREFACE
TO THE FIRST EDITION

THIS volume owes its existence to the generosity of a former pupil, Mr James Fairbairn. Anxious that each boy should take with him some record of the life of his *Alma Mater*, Mr Fairbairn undertook to provide a copy for all pupils leaving School during the next decade. It is peculiarly appropriate to a School steeped, as ours is, in the classical tradition, that one of her sons should have volunteered this λειτουργία.

For the making of the book, I would first acknowledge my debt to my predecessors, Dr Steven and Mr J. J. Trotter. I would further make grateful recognition of the help received from my colleagues and from officials of the various School Clubs. I am particularly indebted to the Rector and to my former Dux, Dr Gordon Donaldson, for reading both manuscript and proofs, and giving me valuable advice.

WILLIAM C. A. ROSS

THE ROYAL HIGH SCHOOL
June 1934

PREFACE
TO THE SECOND EDITION

WHEN the first edition of this book was exhausted, the Royal High School Club undertook to finance a Second Edition in order to continue the gift which Mr. Fairbairn had made to boys leaving School. This generous decision has given me the opportunity of correcting errors and omissions, of bringing the record up to date and of joining those who served in 1939-1945 with their predecessors in the Dedication.

WILLIAM C. A. ROSS

THE ROYAL HIGH SCHOOL
March 1949

CONTENTS

ILLUSTRATIONS

INTRODUCTORY

THIS book makes no pretension to be a formal History of the School. Indeed, the materials for such a work do not exist. Practically nothing survives from pre-Reformation times. After the School passes into the hands of the Town Council there are, of course, the minutes of that body, dealing with the administrative side, but often throwing a sidelight on other matters. Casually, in unexpected places, we may get a reference to the School. But there are large gaps which can never be filled. To some extent this is due to the nature of grammar schools from the sixteenth to the nineteenth centuries. The Town Council owned and upkept the buildings, laid down the course of study, and the regulations for discipline, appointed the Rector and masters, paid them salaries somewhat in the nature of token payments,[1] and fixed the fees. But the masters collected and retained the fees of their respective

[1] *E.g.* In the session 1827-28 Benjamin Mackay drew £700 in fees. His salary, like that of other masters, was £20.

classes. Their class registers were their account books, so there was no thought of preserving them in the School. The numbers in a class mattered primarily to the master of that class. To the Town it was mainly a question of the prestige of the School, not of income; indeed, it might be a question of expenditure. From time to time the masters petition for an increase of salary, and sometimes the ground is that the numbers have gone down. It is in this casual way that now and again we get an inkling of how the numbers stand. Anything like a continuous record of the enrolment before 1739 is out of the question. Even between 1739 and 1827 we are dependent on the Library Registers, which record all the boys who paid a Library fee, but not necessarily all the boys who were enrolled. It is not till 1827 that our first Matriculation Register begins. Even then the information—name and class—is not particularly helpful. The first published Rector's Report (1846) is really the beginning of continuous historical material. We cannot even tell when or how the name "High School" was changed to "Royal High School." James VI. and I. spoke of *Schola Regia*, but the English version is of later date. It is to be found on the map of the Edinburgh Directory of 1833-34 but its general use seems to date

2

from about 1867. There we must leave it in the hope that further evidence may some day come to light.

Some aspects of the School's life which are capable of continuous treatment are sketched in the following chapters. Here I shall deal with episodes in the School's history which link up with the life of the times.

.   .   .   .   .

Religion has played a large part in the history of Scotland, and it is not inappropriate that our first incident should be connected with the ecclesiastical disputes of the sixteenth century. At the time of the Reformation the Rector was William Robertoun, whom his opponents describe as " ane obstinate Papeist," and also as a man of slight erudition. In 1565 the Magistrates dismissed him from office. But Robertoun appealed to Queen Mary, who ordered the Council " to thole him peaceably brook and enjoy his office during his lifetime," and they had to take him back and also pay up all his arrears of salary. In May 1568, however, after the Battle of Langside, having lost his protectress, he consented to retire on pension. But he made things so uncomfortable for his successor, Thomas Buchanan, a nephew of the famous George, that Thomas resigned in 1571, whereupon the obstinate Robertoun jumped into the saddle again. As Kirkaldy of Grange held the Castle for Queen Mary in 1571, and as Buchanan was promptly made Rector of the Grammar School of Stirling, where Mary's opponents had their headquarters, it is reasonable to assume that politics entered into both moves. With Kirkaldy's guns trained on the city the Magistrates would have more to think about than petty scholastic squabbles. Probably, too, there would be a section of the Council secretly at least in half sympathy with the old Faith in which they had been brought up. At any rate, Robertoun kept his seat till 1584, when he once more and finally retired on pension. There was strong anti-Catholic feeling about this time.

Robertoun was not the only master to suffer for his religious convictions. At a later date, in 1679—the year of the murder of Archbishop Sharp, of Drumclog, and of Bothwell Brig— when Episcopacy was in the ascendant, the Rector, Alexander Heriot, and one of the masters, James Scott, were deposed for refusing to recognise " the government of the Church by Archbishops and Bishops."

.   .   .   .   .

Every High School boy, whatever else he may or may not know, knows two things: that Walter Scott was a High School boy, and that

his predecessors once shot a Bailie. Adhering
to chronological order, let us take the latter
case first.

To-day, should the boys of the School desire
a holiday, the Captain of the School would duly
prefer their request to the Rector. The custom
of a ruder age was otherwise. The " barring
out " was not a singular phenomenon; it was
the conventional method whereby the scholars
signified their desire for a relaxation from their
labours. The first move was to approach the
Council with a request for a " privilege " (*i.e.*
holiday). The recognised reply to this gambit
was a negative response. Then the bolder
spirits, armed with lethal weapons and sus-
tained by a store of provisions, occupied the
school during the night. Barring the doors,
they prepared to stand a siege till either their
request was granted or the fortress was stormed.
Several cases are recorded in the years preceding
the McMorane episode. In 1580 one led to
nine of the scholars being imprisoned and fined.
A few years later (1587) another occurred.
When the Magistrates, headed by Lord Provost
William Little, eventually forced an entrance,
they found the garrison armed with firearms
of every description, with swords and with
halberds. Fortunately, the boys do not seem to
have used their weapons. All that they gained on

this occasion, besides individual punishment by fine, was a curtailment of the annual vacation.

The " barring out " of 1595 owes its notoriety to the tragic fate of Bailie John McMorane. Curiously enough, the Bailie figures three years earlier in the life of the School, when he obtains a contract " to big a loft for the warding of the scholars," and his brother Ninian is one of the Committee appointed in 1594 to visit and report on the School. It may be that the boys bore a grudge against the McMorane family, or it may only be that William Sinclair, son of the Chancellor of Caithness, was as much of a dare-devil as other Caithness Sinclairs were at this period of Scottish history. At any rate, on this occasion the boys not only had weapons but used them.

When the Bailie and the Town's officers arrived they were refused admission, whereupon they took up a joist and started to " ding doun " the back door. Sinclair bade them desist, calling them " buttery carles," and vowing that he would put a bullet through their brains. The unfortunate Bailie did not believe that the boy would carry out his threat and continued to " ding the door," whereupon Sinclair shot him through the head.[1]

[1] The School Play of 1948, "Authors of Mischief", written by W. D. Platt (VI.U) and K. F. C. Miller (V.A) was based on this incident.

THE HIGH SCHOOL, 1578.

It was an awkward business for King James, who, when he got the news at Falkland, must have cursed the day that his *Schola Regia* was born. He could not offend the burgesses of the Good Town, who had given him money before and might do so again. Still less could he offend the turbulent nobility of Scotland, who would never allow " gentilmen's bairns " to suffer for such a venial offence as slaying a mere citizen. As usual he temporised. The infuriated citizens had lodged the young ruffians in the Tolbooth. There they were allowed to cool their heels for a month or two and then released. Their only punishment appears to have been expulsion from the School, a penalty hardly likely to have caused them bitter anguish. The Council, however, had other victims at hand. The Rector was dismissed, and the masters were docked of their salaries, which, in all the circumstances of the case, seems rather hard luck.

We do not hear of " barrings out " after this period, but that is no evidence that the spirit of riotousness had been exorcised from the High School. More than a hundred years later, in 1716, the boys broke all the windows of the School and of Lady Yester's Church, and levelled to the ground the wall that surrounded the playground. What moved them to this

7

outburst, and what penalty they incurred, are alike concealed from us. Was it some aftermath of the '15? The story of the School leaves much to the imagination.

.　　.　　.　　.　　.

The warlike propensities of the pupils found another outlet in the " bicker." The earliest recorded one concerns a celebrated figure in Scottish history—" Tam o' the Cowgate," first Earl of Haddington, Lord President of the Court of Session and a great friend of James VI. His house was in Merchant's Court, where the south piers of George IV. Bridge now stand. The story goes that one day, sitting at his ease after dinner in dressing-gown and slippers, he heard the tumult of a bicker between School and College. These frays, when sticks and stones were freely used and crowns were cracked, were no ploy for an old man; but the Earl was a High School boy; he owed no allegiance to the College, for he had gone from School to Paris. Down the stair he rushed. Castor and Pollux at Lake Regillus were not more unexpected, more welcome, or more effective than was this stout-hearted old man in the Cowgate of Edinburgh. He rallied his hard-pressed schoolmates and led them to victory. The College lads were driven through the Grassmarket and clean out of the town at

the West Port. Tam consolidated his victory by getting the gate shut and barred, and then returned triumphant, and probably somewhat breathless, to his wine.

In 1660 there is a quaint note in the Council Record: " Compeared Mr John Home, master of the Grammar School, and complained upon John Mushet and John McClure, two of Mr Thomas Blackburn's scholars for seducing of the said Mr John his scholars to the bickering." It is unlikely, *pace* Mr Home, that much seduction was required. Thomas Blackburn was probably the master of one of the private schools, against which both High School masters and Town Council fulminate from time to time.

This form of amusement persisted for a long time. Scott has immortalised it in the story of " Green-Breeks," and another former pupil, George Borrow, gives, in *Lavengro*, a vivid picture of one in which he was engaged. But it would be wrong to suppose that High School boys spent all the time they could spare from Latin in breaking windows or cracking crowns. I do not suppose they were really very different from ourselves. For one thing, they imitated their elders, and that is still the fashion; for another they had not the same outlets for their physical energy that we now possess. Bicker and " barring out " have given place to cricket and football—and sometimes the latter, at any rate, does not seem so very different. And there was just as good a spirit of sportsmanship in these old frays— witness the story of " Green-Breeks."

.　　.　　.　　.　　.

Another way in which we find the events of the day affecting the life of the School is in the domain of public health. From time to time we read of the School being closed owing to pestilence. Epidemic diseases were frequent in the days when scant reverence was paid to the goddess Hygeia. In 1598 the Council paid compensation to the masters for loss of fees owing to the closing of the School from this cause. On 16th April 1645 the School was " dissolved " till 20th May. As the College was at the same time dissolved " through the occasion of the imminent danger of contagion," we may assume that the same cause operated in both cases. When we find in 1641 the Council ordering the waste ground at the High School Yards to be inspected to see if it would do for the use of the fleshers, we get a glimpse of the sanitary standards of the day.

.　　.　　.　　.　　.

I have referred elsewhere to the effects of Cromwell's visit (p. 25) and of the Treaty of

Union (p. 25). The '15 and the '45 must also have had their repercussions. Perhaps the former can claim the incident at Lady Yester's Church, already referred to; the only trace of the latter I have discovered is the story of John McLure, who was writing master from 1737 to 1777. During the '45, John became attached to the forces of George II. in some unspecified capacity, and was present at the Battle of Falkirk. Like many others he ran away, but was captured by the Jacobites. From the start he seems to have had little confidence in either his own or his general's military ability, for when his captors came to strip him they found under his waistcoat a paper, on which was written: " This is the body of John McLure, writing master in Edinburgh; whoever finds the same is requested to give it Christian burial." May we claim John as the inventor of the identity disc? At any rate, this specimen of John's caligraphy saved his life and he returned to his civil employment, only to run away again in 1777 and so miss the chance of teaching Walter Scott writing—a privilege which fell to Edmond Butterworth.

. . . . .

The close of the eighteenth and opening of the nineteenth centuries were for Edinburgh the Augustan age in literature. This is the period of the School's history with which the general public is best acquainted. Walter Scott stood head and shoulders above his literary contemporaries; the Rector, Alexander Adam, held a similar position in his own profession. Scott's most recent biographer, Mr John Buchan, suggests that Scott got little from the class-rooms of the High School. It may be so; though the description of Luke Fraser as " no more than a grammarian " is merely a flight of imagination. Scott himself, it is true, in his Autobiography, appears to lend some colour to the view that he did not learn much. But it requires little acquaintance with old boys to realise that none of them ever did any work at school, and the more distinguished they are the less apparently they exerted themselves in youth. It is left to their biographers to unearth the details of their successes. Scott tells us " on the whole I made a brighter figure in the *yards* than in the *class*." Who is there to-day who does not look back with more pride on a 1st XV. cap than on a Dux Medal?

I cannot, as one could do nowadays, give you Scott's class place and percentage—not that these would matter in the least. We have his own word for it that he worked for Adam and was stimulated by the work.

Indeed, it is impossible to imagine anyone of Scott's nature and gifts failing to respond to such a stimulus. For the rest, all we know is something of the books he read while a pupil, as recorded in our Library Registers: Langhorne's *Plutarch*, Robertson's *History of Scotland*, Goldsmith's *Greece*, Goldsmith's *England*, *The World Displayed*, *The Annual Register*, Sully's *Memoirs*, and all the Voyages and Travels which were then in the Library. Perhaps this was just a reaction from the tedium of a mere " grammarian's " class-room.

The Borders are a breeding ground of poetry and romance. Every Borderer is a potential poet. Scott was essentially a Border Laird with the gift of expressing his thoughts in words. He had two advantages over his contemporary, the Ettrick Shepherd—greater genius and a wider education. The foundations of the latter were laid at the High School of Edinburgh. With this contribution to the making of Walter Scott we can be content.

.　　.　　.　　.　　.

History makes it clear that from early times our Scottish monarchs took an interest in education. Their gifts to the Church were indirect endowments of learning. Two at least—Aberdeen and Edinburgh—of the four

Universities that Scotland possessed before 1603 owed their existence largely to royal encouragement. James IV., the renaissance King of Scotland, in 1496 enacted that all barons and freeholders should send their sons to grammar schools and keep them there till they had acquired " perfect Latyn." But it does not appear that example was combined with precept. We have no record that either he or any of his forbears or descendants sent their offspring to grammar schools. So we cannot claim to have had a hand in the education of a royal prince till H.R.H. the Prince of Wales came in the summer of 1859 to reside at Holyrood and to study Roman History under the Rector, Dr Schmitz.

Our other royal pupils were of foreign stock. The French Revolution of 1830 gave Louis Philippe a throne. That of 1848 took it away again. Holyrood had given a refuge to his predecessor, Charles X. Once again the Scottish capital gave shelter to exiles from the " auld ally," and scions of her royal race sat on the benches of the School. And it would appear that they were not unapt pupils. Amongst the names read out on Prize Day 1860 were those of their Royal Highnesses Ferdinand d'Orléans, Duc d'Alençon; Louis d'Orléans, Prince de Condé: and Pierre d'Orléans, Duc de Penthièvre. Scotland owes much to the cultural influence of France, and it is pleasant to think that it fell to us to make this slight return.

.   .   .   .   .

In recent years the School has been honoured by a succession of Royal visits. King Edward and Queen Alexandra received a loyal address at the main entrance to the School in May 1903, His Majesty thus renewing acquaintance with the School where, when Prince of Wales, he presented the Carson Medal in 1859. The portico and the walls facing Regent Road make an admirable setting for such a ceremony, and they and the pavement in front were crowded with parents and former and present pupils, who gave their Majesties a royal welcome.

In July 1919 we were similarly honoured by H.R.H. the Prince of Wales. Few who were present will forget the hearty handshake with which His Royal Highness greeted the Captain of the School. With all due respect to the grave and reverend seignors who formed the bulk of the reception party we felt that the Prince's sympathies were obviously with boys, and we cheered him accordingly.

H.I.H. the Crown Prince of Japan, later the Mikado Hirohito, visited the school in May 1921. After inspecting the work of the various departments he was formally welcomed in Hall and graciously accepted a copy of the Roll of Honour. Before his departure the School Choir sang the Japanese National Anthem " Kimigayo." This was the first occasion on which His Imperial Highness had heard his National Anthem sung in this country.

In July 1925 H.R.H. the Prince Henry visited the School. He then proceeded to the Memorial Field at Jock's Lodge, where he opened the Pavilion presented by the Education Authority. After the opening ceremony, His Royal Highness planted a commemorative tree in the entrance grounds of the field. On this occasion he was graciously pleased to accept a copy of the Roll of Honour and of Mr Trotter's History of the School, and to permit himself to be enrolled among the Honorary Life Members of the Athletic Club.

Our latest Royal visitor, Sir Ofori Atta, Paramount Chief of the Gold Coast, came in July 1925. His burly figure, his resplendent purple robes, his wealth of rings and bracelets, and above all his golden crown made a great, impression, particularly on the younger boys, while his speech, fluently delivered in faultless English, was warmly received.

So, for the time being, the tale is complete:

doubtless subsequent chroniclers will have occasion to add to it. For their benefit, if for no other reason, let us record that all these visitors obtained for us the old time " privilege " so dear to the schoolboy heart—a holiday.

.   .   .   .   .

My predecessors have given lists of eminent former pupils. Limits of space preclude me from following their example, but some reference must be made to those who, in after life, have shed lustre on their *Alma Mater*. " ' The tree must be judged by its fruits ' is a maxim which is perhaps more applicable to a school than to any other institution; nay, it is almost the only test by which the efficiency of a school can be rightly judged." So runs the opening sentence of Dr Schmitz's *Annual Report* for the year 1852-3. It is a sound claim if we read it aright. The purpose of a school is to fit its pupils for life. If the work is well done its old boys will be good and useful citizens—but they will not necessarily be distinguished. The panels bearing the names of 314 old boys who gave their lives at the call of duty are as clear a testimony that the work of the School is well done, as are the portraits of illustrious men which adorn our walls.

But all schools are proud, and naturally so, of those of their former pupils who attain to eminence. In the case of an old School such as ours the list, could we make it complete, would inevitably be a long one. But early records take little note of where men were educated. It is casual reference that enables us to identify such men as Drummond of Hawthornden or Tam o' the Cowgate as former pupils. We know that in more recent times we can claim many Moderators of the Scottish Churches, an Archbishop of Canterbury, an Archbishop of York, a Roman Catholic Archbishop of St Andrews and Edinburgh, three Lord Chancellors, many Lord Provosts of the City, Senators of the College of Justice, and Professors of the University, as well as sailors, soldiers, statesmen, poets, painters, inventors, and indeed men eminent in every walk of life. The Annual *Prospectus* records some of the numerous names, and to that publication I must refer my readers.

.   .   .   .   .

There is one School ceremony that is unique in character. No one who was present at the Dedication of the Memorial Porch will ever forget that supreme moment when, as the last notes of Reveille died away, the Memorial Door was opened wide and a flood of sunshine poured into the Hall. Was it then that the idea was born? Year by year, at the close of

Prize Day, the senior boys say farewell to the Rector and pass through that Memorial Door into the world outside, to be welcomed there by a representative of the Former Pupil's Club. It is the crown of a school career, the perfect symbol of that unity of past and present which is our glorious heritage.

HABITATIONS OF THE SCHOOL

It has been generally assumed that the earliest habitation of the School was within the precincts of the now ruined Abbey of Holyrood. Dr Hay Fleming, however, has suggested that the School existed prior to the foundation of the Abbey. "As the appointment of the Master of the Grammar School," he says, " lay with the Abbot and Chapter of Holyrood, it has been inferred that David the First's grant of the Churches of the Castle and of St Cuthbert's of Edinburgh carried, though it did not name, the school of Edinburgh to the Canons of Holyrood." Professor Hannay thinks it probable that the Augustinian canons, for whom Holyrood was built, had acquired the patronage of the School while their residence was still in the Castle, as was the case before they went to Holyrood. But where the School building was situated, either before or after the foundation of Holyrood, is quite unknown.

The earliest definite reference to School premises that I have been able to trace is in an Instrument of Sasine, dated 1503, where there

is mention of " terram scolae grammaticae."
In another, of 1505, there is a reference to
" summa scola grammatica," apparently the
first-recorded use of the title " High School."
The property referred to is described as being
situated in the Vennel of the Church of
St Mary in the Fields.

In 1516, David Vocat, Rector of the School,
dispones to the Town this schoolhouse,
described as situated in " the Kirk o' Field
Wynd, in the eist part of the trans thereof."
This " trans " has been identified with the
High School Wynd of later days. We have no
means of knowing how the schoolhouse came
to be apparently the private property of the
Rector, but it now passes into the hands of the
Town Council, where it has since remained.
The Council does not appear to have looked
after its property very well, for in 1552 it is
described as " now waist and fallen doun."
In this condition it continued, so far as we
know, to be used for educational purposes for
another three years. It is true that in 1554
the " Thesaurer " was ordained " sa soon and
gudlie as he may caus big the Grammar Skule
lyand on the eist side of the Kirk o' Field
Wynd," but he seems to have been in no
hurry, for in the next year the Council leased
from John Betoun of Capildra " the haill

luging lyand at the fute of the Blackfreir Wynd, within the cloiss thairof," for the use of the Grammar School. This was the building commonly known as Cardinal Beaton's Palace.

The School was unfortunate in its premises in these days. In 1569 " the baillies and counsall understand the Bischop of Sanct Andres luging in the Freir Wynd, where presentlie is the grammar schole, to be sa ruynous that the samyn shall nocht be habitable for the wynter following without the greit danger and perell of the bairnis. Quhairfor they ordainis Andro Stevenson, thesaurer, with all diligence possible to repair and mend in fluring, wyndois and utheris necessaries the luging in the Kirkyaird callit the Provost's luging with desks and saitis convenient for the maister of the grammar scole to teach the bairnis thereintill." This Provost's lodging was perhaps the place referred to in a charter dated 1496, by which William Forbes, Provost of the Collegiate Church of St Giles, made over a part of his manse and glebe to the Town. " Know ye us . . . to have given . . . all and whole that north part of our mansion and glebe . . . for which the Provost, Bailies, Councillors and Community of the said Burg . . . are held bound to build a new convenient chamber for the curate and a suitable school below the same . . . in the place where it now is." On the other hand, it may have belonged to the Collegiate Church of St Mary in the Fields. What happened in 1569 to the occupants of this lodging, or whether the Reformation had caused it to be left derelict, we cannot tell; but the High School certainly left the Cardinal's Palace, for in this year the Council paid John Sandilands, "parson of Hawick," all arrears of rent and delivered to him the keys.

The new abode, wherever it was, proved no more satisfactory than its predecessor had been, for in 1577 the Council "understandand themselves to be debtbound in great mailis to Archibald Stewart and his wyf for their Hie Scole, quhilk was nicht wattertycht, wyndtycht, nor lokfast," gave orders for its repair. In a later minute Stewart is described as Provost, but of what is not stated.

Possibly the Council's habit of being in arrears with the rent had some connection with the state of disrepair which seems to have been chronic in their School buildings. At any rate, they apparently got tired of owing money and executing repairs on other people's property. So in February 1578 they hark back to their decision of 1554 and "ordainis James Ros, thesaurer, with all diligence possible to begin

23

found and big the Hie Scole in the maist
commodeous place within the Blackfreir Kirkyaird, and be sa diligent thereupon that the
samyn may be compleit bigit for the resaving
of the youth betuix and Whitsonday next."

What the total cost of this School was is not
recorded, but the contract for the mason work
alone was for £260. This did not include the
boundary wall, nor the roof, nor, of course, the
plenishing. And, if we may judge by the
accounts for the building of 1825, the contract
price would be exceeded. The funds were
raised by " an extent on the inhabitants " (*i.e.* a
special rate was levied for the purpose).

This building, completed in 1578, was the
first, so far as we know, that was definitely
built for the purpose of housing the " Hie
Scole," and it remained in use for two hundred
years, with from time to time modifications of
its internal structure. The most important of
these was made shortly after it was built.
When the system of four regents was introduced
in 1598 (*see* p. 42), the Council decreed that
" ilk ane of the four regentis sall teach their
class in several howsiss (*i.e.* separate class-
rooms) and to this effect the Hie Scole sall be
devydit in four houssis by three parpennis
(partitions)."

Between 1650 and 1658 there was a tempo-

Royal High School, Edinburgh.

Arthur C. Robertson.

rary interruption of its use as a School. When that rude disturber of scholastic peace, Oliver Cromwell, took possession of Edinburgh after the Battle of Dunbar, he ejected the scholars and turned the building into a barracks. His godly troopers occupied it for several years and left it in a state of total disrepair, thus demonstrating that, however godly, they were none the less troopers. The Council ordained that the expense of the repairs, which cost £100, was to be met out of the funds of the Hospital at the foot of Leith Walk " as a work of piety and charity." Meantime the School had been conducted in Lady Yester's Kirk, and in June 1658 there was a formal procession of Magistrates and scholars from the Kirk back to the renovated School.

On the whole this building, erected originally to hold all the pupils in one large room, with a hall below, and subsequently subdivided, did uncommonly well to serve for two hundred years. But the population was growing, though slowly, and possibly a new building would have been required sooner but for the Union of 1707. Arbuthnot, who was Rector from 1717 to 1735, notes in 1718 that the numbers attending the School have greatly diminished. " There are now," he says, " scarce any of the nobility and very few of the gentlemen of the country residing in Edinburgh, and the youth who attend my instructions are almost altogether the children of burgesses." Time, as our records show, was to remedy a state of affairs which undoubtedly contributed to making the building adequate for a longer period than would otherwise have been the case. By 1775, however, it was clear that the old building was inadequate. So, too, were the city funds, and recourse was had to a public subscription, which raised £2300, of which the Council subscribed 300 guineas. Eventually the New School cost over £4000, and, of course, the Council had ultimately to meet the bill. This they did by various expedients, such as granting for a period of years the income from an annual benefit performance at the Theatre Royal (to which, by its contract with the " patentee " the Town was entitled), and by paying £200 annually to the Committee of Subscribers till the whole expense had been met. They presumably hoped that more subscriptions would be gathered in, and this may have happened. The books of the Committee of Subscribers do not survive. The last payment by the Town was made in 1790.

The old School had run east and west, and in spite of slight additions to the area, which were acquired at this time, it was necessary to build the new School partly on the site of the old. To effect this purpose the west end of the old School, containing two class-rooms, was pulled down, these classes being temporarily accommodated in the hall underneath the other three classes. (After the institution of a fifth class in 1614 an extra class-room was required.) The new building thus ran from north to south across the west end of the old one. On the ground floor it contained the Great Hall and two side-rooms—the library and the writing-room. Above were five class-rooms reached by three separate staircases projecting from the back of the Great Hall. The foundation-stone was laid on 24th June 1777, with the usual Masonic ceremonial. Sir William Forbes, the eminent banker, who was Chairman of the Committee of Subscribers, was also at that time Grand Master Mason of Scotland. The reporter of the *Caledonian Mercury* grew lyrical over the " charming spectacle of above 350 fine boys " and dilated upon the importance of " spacious lofty apartments for the accommodation of so very promising a race of young gentlemen." Little did he dream that in two years this promising company would be joined by one who far outstripped them all, to wit, Walter Scott.

We know the date on which the foundation-

stone was laid: when the building was opened
we cannot say. The most probable assumption
is that it was built and put into use piecemeal.
In 1780, Sir William Forbes asks the Town
Council to assign the profits mentioned above
(from the theatrical performances) to the
Committee of Subscribers, who " will proceed
gradually in completing what is still necessary."
In the same year we find the writing master,
Edmond Butterworth, advertising his classes
in a separate building, as his room is not yet
ready. The Great Hall was certainly complete
before 1782, for in that year David, Earl of
Buchan, brother of Lord Chancellor Erskine,
delivered a Latin oration there to the boys,
who were doubtless much edified. As Walter
Scott went to the School in 1779, it seems clear
that for at least part of his time he must have
been in the original building. Is it fanciful to
suppose that this building, with its two hundred
year old tradition, the building which had
witnessed the slaying of John McMorane, and
which still had its " Bailie's window," left *its*
impress on the mind of Walter Scott, whatever
he may or may not have picked up in the
class-room?

The " spacious and lofty apartments " of the
new building seemed at the time to have
provided ample accommodation for the future.

But those who planned it had not realised what would be the result of another building commenced some ten years before the new School was undertaken. The North Bridge, which spanned the valley of the Nor' Loch, opened the way for the building of the New Town. Population all over the country was growing rapidly, and new ideas of hygiene were inducing people to move out of the old, crowded, insanitary mediaeval city to more roomy quarters. Naturally, it was the well-to-do classes who led the van. So the parents of many of the pupils found themselves living farther and farther away from the School. They began to complain of the distance and " inconvenience of the way . . . along one of the most crowded thoroughfares of the city." They must also, I think, have complained of the crowded class-rooms. In 1820 the School reached its maximum enrolment—890 pupils— while three years later the Rector's class consisted of 257 boys.

The Council, in accordance with use and wont, pursued a policy of masterly inactivity. There was the more reason for this, inasmuch as the funds of the Town were in a perilous position. The city was heading fast for that reef of bankruptcy on which she later struck. But that, of course, was not going to satisfy those who desired adequate provision for the education of their children, and while the Council sat tight the public moved. A body of eminent citizens formed themselves into a Committee for the erection of a New Academy on the north side of the town. Cockburn, in his *Memorials*, gives his account of the inception of this scheme. He tells how, " on the top of one of the Pentlands, emblematic of the solidity of our foundations, we two (Leonard Horner and himself) resolved to set about the establishment of a new School."

The Council now realised that something would have to be done, as they were most unwilling to see a new school started outwith their control. At first they proposed to build the new school themselves, and to maintain two High Schools, one in the Old Town and one in the New. To this the contributors to the scheme for a new school were prepared to agree. Their minutes for 10th July 1822 bear that " on an explicit and unqualified determination being intimated by the Lord Provost, Magistrates and Council to proceed without delay in terms of the Report of the Sub-Committee, . . . the scheme of the subscribers shall be abandoned." In reply to this the Council " do now resolve to proceed with the erection of an additional school connected with

and precisely on the footing of the High
School." But there were two parties in the
Council: one, led by the Lord Provost, in
favour of two schools, the other, led by Old
(*i.e.* ex-) Bailie Blackwood, in favour of one
central school. The point on which both
parties agreed was that the control of education
must be in the hands of the Town Council. At
first the Lord Provost's party had it all their
own way, but Old Bailie Blackwood was
evidently a tenacious man. He stuck to his
guns, took full advantage of financial difficulties to delay action, and finally gained his
point. Starting the battle in a minority of
four to nineteen, he ultimately carried his
resolution by a majority of sixteen to eleven.
Whether he was well advised or not is open to
question; one cannot but admire his courage
and pertinacity.

Naturally, the contributors to the New
Academy, incensed at this breach of faith,
broke off negotiations and proceeded with their
own scheme. The Council, being committed
to the idea of a central school, had now to find
the money and the site. Several sites were
considered, the principal being the present site
on the side of the Calton Hill, the Mound,
where the National Gallery now stands, and
the Excise Office, now the home of the Royal

Bank of Scotland. Plans for building on the last-named site were prepared by Thomas Hamilton, and are now in the possession of the School. As we know, the choice ultimately fell on the Calton site, and then arose a pamphleteering war as intense as that which had been waged over the question of two schools or one. The principal argument against the site was the danger of the pupils falling over " the precipices behind the school." The arguments in favour dwelt on the unrivalled views and the " salubrious air," a delicate euphemism for that snell east wind which greets us on a winter's morning. One argument, however, which perhaps weighed more with the Council, though it made little appeal to the pamphleteers, was that the Calton site was town property, so the expense of purchasing a site was saved. On 27th April 1825 it was "moved and unanimously agreed that the ground on the east side of the Baxter's or Miller's Knowe, and on the north of the Calton (now Regent) Road was the most suitable site for a new High School, and the same was therefore set apart for that purpose—the present teachers of the High School having expressed their entire approbation of the site." The Baxter's Knowe, which was removed in the course of the levelling operations, was where the janitor's house now stands.

The site being thus fixed, the Council tackled the financial question. They appointed Thomas Hamilton to prepare a plan and expressed the opinion that " the expense should on no account exceed £20,000, including boundary walls, levelling and all other charges; that the Town should give the site of the new School, the produce of the present School and its site, and a certain sum of money not exceeding on any account one or two thousand pounds, relying that the public will come forward with subscriptions for the balance, without which it is impossible to expect that the School can be built in a style suitable to the situation and the object." After spending a year, not very successfully, in collecting subscriptions, the Council accepted an estimate of £16,590, and went on with the work. The original contractor failed, and the remainder of the work had to be let to a new contractor at an enhanced price. No allowance had apparently been made for levelling, walls, railings, furnishings or architect's fees. The upshot of the whole matter was that the bill came to £33,970 3s. 9d. Subscriptions amounted to £4,820 15s. 1d., and the " produce " of the old site and buildings to £7276 2s. 10d.—in all, £12,096 17s. 11d.— leaving the Council to meet an expenditure of £21,873 5s. 10d., instead of the modest " one or at most two thousand pounds " of their original resolution. At least one gleam of humour enlivens these rather depressing financial records. When the first contractor failed, his successor offered to take the scaffolding off his hands. But the price did not please the agent for the bankrupt's creditors, and he wrote: " Though the creditors are anxious to make every sacrifice to second the wishes of the Council, it cannot be expected that they should do so *at their own expense* " —surely an unique example of vicarious sacrifice.

The magnificent buildings financed in this haphazard manner consisted of the main School and the " temples " or lodges at either end, the western lodge being used as the janitor's house. With slight exception the stonework has stood the test of a hundred years. Unlike the rest of the building, which is good Craigleith, the pavement of the portico was laid with Arbroath stone. In 1841 it was reported that there was a subsiding of the portico due to " the total decay of the soft Arbroath stone within the same, so that rain gets through the arches and into the passage below." The portico was immediately " repaved with the very best Craigleith stone, clean polished and finely jointed." At the same time, it was noted that " the honeysuckle

34

ornaments along the eaves of the centre building were falling off." They were consequently all taken down and laid aside till good weather, when they were put up again with strong cement. Internally the main building remains practically as it was built. The " temples," however, have undergone several internal structural alterations. That to the east, after long service as a science department, did duty, not very efficiently, as a refectory. When the much-needed new lunch-room was built this eastern lodge became a home of the technical subjects department. The western lodge has had an even more varied career. Starting as a janitor's lodge, it became in 1885 a swimming bath. Ten years later it was a workshop, and now it is a class-room, with the lethal equipment of the C.C.F. concealed in the crypt.

But additional buildings from time to time have clustered round this nucleus, as modern demands have rendered the original accom-modation inadequate. The first of these were erected in 1885, when the present janitor's lodge was built at the west end of the playground. At the same time a one-storey range of build-ings was erected at the north-east end of the playground, containing the present gymnasium, and a writing-room where the present swimming bath is. Further extension took place in 1895, when additional rooms were built on to the west end of the gymnasium, and an additional storey added to the whole of that building, thus largely increasing the accommodation. At the same time, the writing-room with its accompanying retiring-room was converted into a swimming bath, and a staff-room built out to accommodate the ladies of the Preparatory Department. The old swimming bath in the west lodge was then gutted out and converted into a workshop, with provision for the wood workers above and the disciples of Vulcan below. The latest addition to the buildings is the Craft Room, built in 1925, at the extreme east end of the playground.

It is the painful duty of the historian to record that during the years 1921-1930 the playground was defaced by wooden huts in which some of the Preparatory and Junior School classes were housed, to the manifest discomfort of themselves and their teachers. It was a case, as has been said of the climate of Valladolid, of " nueve meses de invierno y tres de infierno." But this purgatorial period was the prelude to brighter days. The growth of the Preparatory and Junior Departments had rendered extension inevitable, and there was no room for extension within the yards.

So we suffered, by no means in silence, while the quest for a site went on. The ultimate choice was exceedingly happy. The authorities acquired the portion of ground lying to the east of our Memorial Field at Jock's Lodge, and there erected in 1930 a building on the most modern lines for the Preparatory and Junior Schools.

We have now traced, as far as possible, the history of the School buildings proper; but any account of the habitations of the School would be incomplete if it left out the Royal High School House. In 1927, No. 24 Royal Terrace was acquired by Dr James Watt, and opened as a Boarding House for boys attending the School, under the charge of Mr and Mrs Dawson. It has already proved its value both to the scholastic and to the athletic sides of School life, and has enabled former pupils furth of Scotland to maintain in a new generation their connection with their *Alma Mater*.

In December 1941 Dr Watt intimated to the Royal High School Committee his intention of handing over the Boarding House to the Club. For this purpose a Royal High School Trust was formed, which was authorised to hold as Trustee any property or funds of the Club, and the House is accordingly vested in it.

Since 1934, there have been further developments on or adjacent to the Regent Road site and also at Jock's Lodge. In 1935 the problem of an adequate Lunch Room for the Senior School was tackled and the present building opposite the Gymnasium was erected. It was a great step forward then, though increasing numbers have made the word adequate less appropriate to-day. But it at least set free the East Lodge to house the Technical subjects.

In 1943 the Library was cleansed of its typewriting desks and refurnished in a manner befitting its noble proportions and its intellectual purpose. We have thus been provided with a fitting place in which to hold School gatherings. It was here that we entertained our returned prisoners of war after the defeats of Germany and of Japan. Here too the Royal High School Club held its first post-war Dinner.

Two years later the pressure of increasing numbers led to the erection at Jock's Lodge of two additional classrooms. The clamant needs of the Senior School were met in the following year by the acquisition of No. 1 Regent Terrace. The Art Department, after wandering like Noah's dove, has at last settled down in reasonable proximity to the Ark, and the Science Department has secured a much-needed extension into what was once the Art Room.

The most important addition to our cultural activities came in the years 1946-1947. We had long dreamt of and even talked about an Organ in the Hall. Thanks to the enthusiasm of Rector Ball and the ready response of Present and Former Pupils, including a grant of £500 by the Royal High School Club from the Burns' Bequest, the dream has come true. The work of installation was admirably carried out by Messrs. Donald Grant and Sons, a firm of Former Pupils to whom we were indebted for the display cabinets which house our Trophies in the Hall.

There are two other matters in hand which will, we hope, be completed by the time this volume is published. Work has started on three new classrooms to the east of the Janitor's Lodge at Regent Road and it is hoped that these will be available next session.

The Windows in the Hall to commemorate our school-fellows who gave their lives in the second World War will be dedicated in July, 1949. These " storied windows, richly dight " and the panels bearing the names of the fallen, we owe to the work of the Ladies' Committee. Under the energetic convenership of Mrs. Ball, they raised the funds to meet the entire cost— surely a notable example of the family tradition in Royal High School life.

THE CHANGING CURRICULUM

THE curriculum of the School has undergone many changes since that April day in 1519, when the Town Council ordained that " no manner of neighbours or indwellers in the Burgh put their bairns to any school except the principal Grammar School, to be teachit grace buke, primer and plane donatt " (the grammar of Aelius Donatus). And yet, with all the changes, are expectations to-day as sanguine as they were four hundred years ago, when Adam Melvill obliged himself " to mak the bairnys perfyte grammarians within three years "? Even the Scottish Education Department does not demand perfection. Somewhere about 50 per cent. will satisfy it.

The educational curriculum appears to have been an ever-present source of trouble throughout the ages. The minutes of the Town Council bear witness to a recurrence of visitations, reports, and plans almost comparable to the distressing frequency of modern Departmental Minutes. It is not always easy, however, to find out exactly what happened. From the year 1584, when certain of the Magistrates are

The Royal High School (Preparatory), 1931

appointed "to convene together on Sunday next at afternoon, with such learned men as may be had in the burgh, to give their advice and judgment and set down the form of a certain course and order of book and lessons to be taught within the said High School," to the day of Government inspection the stream is steady. But the Council scribe for the time being, while sedulously recording the appointment, seems frequently to have regarded the report as unworthy of a similar attention; and we are left wondering what came of it all. Probably then, as now, the masters got on with their job and paid little attention to the windy paper snowstorms that whirled about their ears. The sane view of the matter was well expressed at a later date by Dr Adam. Writing to the Rector of Aberdeen Grammar School, he says, " For magistrates to impose or give absurd regulations how you are to conduct the education of your boys, I should think it rather stepping beyond their sphere. Their intervention ought to go no further than advice and support. I have at different times experienced the hurtful effects of such interference."

No detailed record of our early curriculum survives, but we may fairly assume that in pre-Reformation times both curriculum and hours would be similar to those of other grammar schools. That is to say, we would study Latin and probably elementary Theology, and we would do this between the hours 7-9, 10-12, 2-5, or perhaps 6, and the holidays would be Saints' days. The Reformation would naturally bring about some changes. We find in the Town Council's contract with Hercules Rollock (1584) that he is " to instruct the youth in pietie, guid maneris, doctrine and letteris "—an admirable programme, unhampered by detail; while five years later he is given power to grant his scholars a " privilege," as a holiday was then called, twice a year—eight days in May and the same in September.

The earliest detailed course of study that has come down to us is dated 1598, and was the work of a committee consisting of a Senator of the College of Justice, six advocates, the Principal of the College (*i.e.* University), the Provost, two bailies, the Dean of Guild, three ministers, and a writer (*i.e.* lawyer). It provides for four " learned and godly men " being appointed to teach the School " in all time coming " in four classes:—

Class I.—The Rudiments of Dunbar; the Colloquies of Corderius; and on Sunday Palatinus.

Class II.—The first part of Pelisso; Cicero's Familiar Epistles; on Sunday the foresaid Catechism lately set out in Latin, with Ovid De Tristibus.

42

Class III.—The second part of Pelisso, with the Supplement of Erasmus Syntaxis; Terence; The Metamorphoses of Ovid, with Buchanan's Psalms on Sunday.

Class IV.—The third part of Pelisso with Buchanan's Prosodia; Taleus Figures and Rhetoric Figure Constructionis Thome Linacri; Vergilius; Salustius; Caesaris Commentaria; Florus; Ovidii Epistolae and the Heroic Psalms of Buchanan on Sunday.

The Regent of Class IV. was to act as Rector. The terms Regent, Doctor or Master appear to be used indifferently. Under this system the Regent did not carry on his class for four years, but remained in charge of the first or second or whatever class he had when appointed. In a later minute the Regent of Class IV. is referred to as the " principal " and the others as " inferior " Regents. There was a difference both in their salaries and in the fees paid by their pupils. When the practice began of a master carrying on a class for four years and then turning it over to the Rector is not clear. It must have been at some date later than 1614, when a fifth class was formed, and earlier than the middle of the eighteenth century, by which time the practice is clearly established.

It will be noted from the above curriculum that the School met on Sundays. Saturdays,

of course, were just like any other days. No
mention is made in this report of any provision
for the teaching of writing, although five years
earlier licence had been granted to William
Murdo to teach writing in the High School,
and a chamber was furnished by the Town
Council for this purpose. And the practice
was kept up, for the appointment of a successor
to Murdo is recorded. But a writing master
was not properly " on the staff." He was a
" visiting master," and there is no record of
his being paid a salary.

" For all time " is but a brief span in
educational programmes. In 1614 the text
books are revised, a fifth class is added, and
the study of Greek is begun. Pelisso makes way
for Despauter. Quintus Curtius, Plautus,
Horace, Juvenal and Persius are pressed into
service, and the fourth and fifth classes are
exercised in verse-making " as their spirit
serves them." Lyesiod or Thergius is prescribed for the teaching of Greek Grammar.
From a later record, the Ordo Scholae Grammaticae Edinensis, prepared in 1644, we
gather that the teaching, after the first class,
was to be conducted as far as possible in the
Latin tongue. We also get the more humane
indication that by this time a month's vacation
in the autumn had crept in.

But before this *Ordo* was drawn up, there appears to have been a lengthening of the school hours. When Thomas Crawford, Professor of Humanity in the College of Edinburgh, was appointed Rector, he became bound " to teach the scholars diligently from six in the morning to nine, and from ten to twelve, and from half-past one in the afternoon till six in the evening," a total of nine and a half hours. When we consider the age at which children went to school in these days, this is as barbarous as anything that the Industrial Revolution produced. It is little wonder that the same inhuman method of flogging the tired horse was employed in both cases. For some reason these hours appear to have been curtailed at a slightly later date. What fanned the latent spark of humanity in the bosom of the Council is not recorded, but its warmth did not thaw the icy heart of Thomas Crawford. In a Memorial to the Council he states " that now in the winter mornings I have too little time to teach the lessons. Wherefore I would pray your wisdoms either to give commandment that our meetings may continue at six hours, or else that all the youth break their fasts before seven and continue in the school till twelve." There must have been joy in the High School when, in 1640, the College from which he had come recalled Crawford to be its Regent in Philosophy and Professor of Mathematics. But he had his good points. In the same Memorial in which he asks for longer hours, he suggests " If it please your wisdoms it will be good to cause some silver pennies or siclike small rewards and tokens to be given to the victors, for *animi praemio ad laborem incenduntur:* and the Council, with the Session of the Kirk, to meet on the last day in the School and to deliver their tokens with some solemnity, which will both encourage the youth and countenance your School." So, in a spirit of charity we may forgive Thomas Crawford for his long hours, which no longer vex us, and remember him gratefully as the originator of our annual Prize Day.

Though not strictly an alteration in the curriculum, the establishment of a Library by Act of Council in 1658, the year in which the School returned from Lady Yester's Church (*see* p. 25) is a memorable step in the educational progress of the School. It is pleasant to record that the Town Council was moved to this commendable step by the representations of the Rector, John Muir. The Council put up the necessary accommodation, and the shelves were furnished with books given by the Rector, masters, pupils, and many of the citizens.

Further changes were introduced in 1696. A Memorial was presented to the Council by parents who complained of the early hours, and the Council resolved that " as many of the inhabitants, whose children are tender, are unwilling to expose them to the cold winter mornings and send them to the said School before the hour of seven, as use is; therefore the Masters of the said School in all time coming (our old friend) shall meet and convene the same at nine of the clock in the morning during the winter season, viz., from the first day of November to the first day of March yearly." At the same time they introduce Wedderburn's Rudiments on the ground that the Latin Rudiments hitherto in use " is difficult and hard for beginners." The worthy Provost who signed this humane ukase was Robert Chieslie. But Robert's judgment was to be upset at an early date. A voluminous Report of 1710 (prepared by a committee consisting of the Reverend Principal Carstares and seven Professors of the College, and adopted by the Council) condemns the fourth part of the grammar in use as being " a confused mass of hard Greek words in Latin characters, containing really nothing which is not much better explained in the Short Compendium of Rhetoric." As to the other three parts,

" Despauter as abridged by Novimola may still be taught until a better is agreed upon." But care must be taken " to pass over in the second part what is false or ridiculous." It would seem that text-books then presented the same problem as they do to-day.

Progress more sure and probably more welcome is made in the provision for a weekly half-holiday: " Every fourth day the scholars to be allowed to play and refresh themselves one whole afternoon, in place of all the other ordinary occasions of dismissing the school, such as the entering of new scholars, the payment of quarter-day payments at the desire of the boy who is victor at Candlemas,[1] or of gentlemen or ladies walking in the yards." This last method of inculcating politeness to one's visitors was doubtless highly appreciated in its day.

In spite of the Report of 1696 there still seems to have been difficulty about the winter hour of assembly. In 1723 the matter is again brought up on a petition from parents that the practice of meeting at seven may be changed during the months from October to February

[1] It was the custom at Candlemas for each boy to present the master with a pecuniary token of esteem. The " victor " was the judicious boy who gave the largest offering. At his request the School was given a holiday as soon as all the contributions had been gathered in.

inclusive. The Rector and masters are consulted. It is good to find them agreeing that the children " will benefit as much by the three uninterrupted hours from nine to twelve as they now do by the four hours seven to nine and ten to twelve." So they are authorised to put the reform into practice.

Geography seems to have been introduced about 1742; in that year the Treasurer is authorised to purchase a pair of globes for the use of the High School.

The biggest storm about text-books was provoked in the reign of that celebrated scholar, Alexander Adam, and gives point to his remarks which we quoted earlier (p. 41). Adam, who had an acknowledged genius for imparting information to boys, as well as inspiring them, found Ruddiman rather tough meat. He published in 1772 a Grammar of his own, and naturally desired to use it. But Adam, excellent and amiable man as he was, appears to have had the faculty of rubbing some people the wrong way. His academic republicanism was obnoxious to the oligarchic Town Council of those days. Many years later, at the Dinner to celebrate the presentation of the Prince of Wales' Bust to the School, Lord Provost Adam Black, speaking of Dr Adam, whom he called the first educational reformer in the School, recalled his habit of asking a boy to tell him the Latin for " King." Getting the answer " Rex," he was wont to say, "Another word? " He then got the word " Tyrannus " (for, of course, the boys knew the game). " Right, boy," was his response. To us it seems a harmless foible, but these were the days of the French Revolution, when to be suspected of Republicanism was on a par with being suspected of Bolshevism to-day—though the conception of Alexander Adam as a potential *sans-culotte* suggests a sad lack of humour in the City Chambers. The controversy over this Grammar went on for several years.

Curiously enough, the masters were unanimously opposed to the Grammar, and declared Ruddiman to be much superior. The position of Rector in those days was no bed of roses. The four Doctors or Masters drew the fees of their own classes. They were largely independent, and clearly at all times intolerant of Rectorial control. In their Memorial (1785) to the Council they " beg leave to hint that so long as *their* labours are so acceptable to the public and *their* classes so well attended, the Rector can never suffer from following the same plan of teaching with them." They also lay great stress on the teaching of Latin in Latin, the head and front of Adam's offence apparently being his reasonable endeavour to make his subject intelligible to those whom he taught. In a letter to the Council he describes his Grammar as " a small book to facilitate the study of Latin by connecting it with the English." Personal rancour, as well as professional jealousy, seems to have crept into this dispute, for the memorialists state that " they heartily approve the plan of school discipline, provided they could see the least probability *at present* of having it carried out with temper, prudence and cordiality." That Willie Nicol, who once assaulted Adam in public, should have signed this amazing document is not surprising; and perhaps Cruickshank, who had been Rector of the Burgh School of the Canongate before he came to the Grammar School of Edinburgh, found it irksome to work under another man. But that French, whose tombstone records that he lived " a life of humility, piety and active benevolence," and still more that the amiable Luke Fraser should have appended their signatures can only be regarded as a singular example of professional solidarity.

The gentle Adam put up a stout fight for his Grammar, but he was worsted. All he could obtain was the right to supplement Ruddiman with observations founded on his own work. He was not to use it as a substitute. We hope and believe that Adam, while constrained formally to bow the knee in the House of Rimmon, remained faithful to the true doctrine, and used Ruddiman as a vehicle for teaching Adam. At some later date, however, he managed to get the book officially recognised, and Dr Steven tells us that it was extensively used both in Britain and in America. His *Roman Antiquities* was even more extensively used, and was for long the standard work on the subject.

In 1781 there had been another change in the hours. Sir William Forbes, on behalf of the Committee of the School and of the Rector and masters, wrote the Council as follows: " It has been thought by many that the hours of attendance in summer are not so well arranged as they may be for the instruction of the boys. In the first place it was believed that it was prejudicial to health as well as not so proper for acquiring knowledge, to fall to study immediately after dinner, and in the second place, by the alteration which time has produced in the hours of dining in the city, it was not possible that the boys can have the benefit of being under their parents' eye and in their company at that meal. These considerations have induced many parents to apply to the Rector and masters to make such an

alteration in the hours of attendance in summer
as that the whole business of the School may be
discussed before three o'clock." The Council
agreed to alter the hours so that school would
finish at three. This change had an unlooked-
for repercussion. Though Adam himself was
gentle and seldom resorted to corporal punishment the general tradition seems to have been
otherwise. Cockburn, in his *Memorials*, gives
a very unfavourable picture of the methods
employed by his particular teacher. The reform
in this practice is ascribed to Adam's successor,
Pillans, by Mr Archibald Carmichael in his
*Recollections of Two Years in the Rector's
Class* (1809-11), where he tells us that Pillans
was responsible for " the substitution of tasks
to be performed at the expense of leisure. . . .
The use of the ancient instruments of correction
in the management of discipline was from that
time greatly discontinued, and in the course of
a few years it was, I am well assured, altogether
superseded." Other evidence leads us to regard
the last statement as somewhat exaggerated.
In any case, it would appear from a letter to the
Caledonian Mercury in May 1781, that the
change—the writer evidently did not regard
it as a reform—began in Dr Adam's time. The
letter, signed "A Parent "—how history antici-
pates itself!—is addressed to the Committee for

the Management of the High School. " When you lately altered the hours of teaching in the High School, I considered myself along with many others obliged to you, as by that alteration I hoped for the pleasure of my son's company to dinner, which I thought an advantage to him and a happiness to myself. But from a new mode of punishment lately adopted by some of the teachers I am so far from finding myself pleased with the change that I wish to God you would give them their old hours again together with the old mode of discipline; for instead of having my son regularly at dinner with me, as I had reason to expect, he has been for six or seven times confined to the School till five o'clock afternoon, and on these occasions arrived home unfit for eating anything whatever. I wish by no means to invalidate the authority of the teacher over his pupils, of the necessity of which I am perfectly satisfied; but I beg leave to put these refined gentlemen in mind of the old mode of punishment practised with equal success and more safety by their forefathers. I flatter myself that the generality of parents will much more cheerfully consent, with me, to the punishing or disgracing of their children during the hours of teaching than to the loss of their appetite, their spirits and their health which must be the effect of confining them in the present cruel and unreasonable manner." History, alas, has not preserved the comments of the erring son on this example of parental tenderness.

Whether Pillans did or did not introduce the practice of infringing on the liberty and leisure of his pupils, he certainly practised and approved of it, and without doubt he introduced to the School and possibly to Scotland the monitorial system as practised by Bell and Lancaster south of the Border. The two things to some extent hang together. With a class ranging between one and two hundred, of very varying abilities, it must have been exceedingly difficult, if not impossible, to secure from all attention and consequently a reasonable measure of discipline. The temptation to fall back on the wisdom of Solomon would be great. But when the master could devote a large part of his time to teaching the abler boys, and could hand over to them some of the work of passing on the torch to their less gifted brethren, his task became less exacting and perhaps his temper more equable. As an adjunct to this monitorial system, Pillans developed, if he did not actually introduce, the system of private study. The maximum amount of work that could be exacted daily from all the class was obviously governed by the capacities of the weaker vessels, and equally obviously would be much too little for the abler boys. Cockburn refers to the " bodily and mental wearisomeness of sitting six hours a day staring idly at a page, without motion and without thought." It was to counter this " wearisomeness " that Pillans encouraged the abler boys to undertake additional work while he was engaged with the lower parts of the class, and from the accounts that survive it is clear that a large amount of reading was got through in this way.

We have seen that the study of Greek was introduced into the curriculum in 1614. In 1820 the Magistrates resolved to set up a special Greek class, to be taught by a Mr Gray, and to inhibit the Rector and masters from teaching that subject. This called forth two protests. One was from Professor Dunbar, who appears to have claimed that the sole right of teaching Greek in Edinburgh belonged to him. His letter was so intemperately worded that the Council resolved that it was " totally undeserving of the notice of the Patrons, discreditable to its author, and ought to be entirely laid out of sight and returned by the Clerk to the Professor." The other was from Bailie Charles, who was apparently the mouth-

ALEXANDER
ADAM, LL.D.
1768 - 1809

JAMES
PILLANS, M.A.
1810 - 1820

AGLIONBY-ROSS
CARSON, LL.D.
1820 - 1845

RECTORS

piece of the masters. He asserted that they had been in the unchallenged practice of teaching Greek for many years, and went on to lay down the constitutional doctrine that " the High School, being a Royal Foundation, the Magistrates, though invested by the Crown with the patronage of the seminary, cannot alter the constitution without the full concurrence of that power to which it owes its existence and they their authority." The prospect of having to get an Act of Parliament, or at the least an Order in Council, for any change in the School's curriculum is rather appalling, but we must not take the good Bailie too seriously. As may be supposed from their treatment of Professor Dunbar's epistle, the Town Council, who were Patrons of both College and School, did nothing to hinder the teaching of Greek in the latter. In 1827 a new " plan of additions to the course of study " was approved. This provided for an optional General Knowledge Class, embracing English Literature, History and Geography, to be taught by the existing masters in their respective classes one hour a day three times a week, and for an optional French Class one hour a day twice a week.

The outline of the course of study is as follows:—

First Year.

   Latin.

   *General Knowledge Class: English Grammar;
     Roman History to the close of the Republic;
     Outline of Modern Geography.

   *French.

Second Year.

   Latin.

   *General Knowledge Class: English Grammar;
     Roman History to the close of the Empire;
     Outline of Ancient Geography.

   *French.

Third Year.

   Latin; Greek; Mythology.

   *General Knowledge Class: English Composition;
     History of Greece to the end of the Pelo-
     ponnesian War; Particular Geography of
     Europe and Asia.

   *French.

Fourth Year.

   Latin; Greek; Roman Antiquities.

   *General Knowledge Class: English Literature
     and Composition; History of Greece till it
     became a Roman Province; Particular Geo-
     graphy of Africa and America.

   *French.

Fifth and Sixth Years.

   " The same course as at present," embracing the
     Higher Greek and Roman Classics with
     Antiquities, Geography and Composition in
     Prose and Verse.

* Optional Subjects.

In spite of the limited amount of time given to the optional subjects, for which, as for writing and arithmetic, an extra fee was charged, this curriculum begins to have a modern ring. The Council published an explanatory address, stating that "without interfering in the slightest degree with the leading department of study, Classical Literature, their object is to introduce into this ancient and celebrated seminary such additional branches as should serve still further to expand the mind, refine the taste, and extend the knowledge of the pupil. . . . The class for General Knowledge cannot fail to prove of the most essential benefit to the intellectual improvement of the pupil, and serve agreeably to diversify, without sensibly augmenting the labours of his classical studies." So, with much flourish of trumpets, perhaps to drown the rumblings of uneasy conscience, the Council give their blessing to the first breach in the ramparts of a rigidly classical education.

In the Report itself there is a quaint paragraph which displays a rather less enlightened spirit. It deals with the status of the writing master, whom apparently the regular masters refuse to recognise as a professional brother. " Respectable as many of the writing masters unquestionably are, it should not be forgotten that it requires no extensive preliminary course of study, no superior endowments of mind, and even no mental exertion whatever to become a skilful and successful teacher of writing." All who are familiar with educational procedure will readily realise that this verbiage was the prelude to cutting down the fees of the " skilful and successful teacher."

From this Report we find that the hours of the School are nine to three in winter and nine to four in summer, " proper intervals being allowed for air and exercise."

This overhaul of 1827 was doubtless dictated in part by the impending removal to new quarters. But the recent celebrations of centenaries by three Edinburgh Schools remind us that other causes were in operation. Competition was looming ahead; the curriculum of one in particular, the Edinburgh Institution (now Melville College) makes it clear that there was a demand for a broader outlook. Whatever the Council might think or wish, clearly the public was not going to stand a purely classical education any longer. And it is the public which supplies the pupils. The Council were loth to move. The masters were torn between the conflicting emotions of devotion to the classics and despair at diminishing fees. We shall see the outcome.

In 1834 there is one of the numerous inquiries into the " causes of decay in the High School." If we may judge by the recurrence of these inquiries, there can be no institution in the universe so like the phoenix as the Royal High School. It is perpetually falling into decay and as regularly rising triumphant from its ashes. Competitors spring up, but whether they go or stay the School continues. The leaves of the tree may wither for a time, but the roots hold firm against the blasts, and soon fresh foliage clothes the branches. This time the foliage took the form of " a French teacher of eminence to teach three hours a day." *Parturiunt montes, nascetur ridiculus mus.*

Another alteration suggested in the next year by Dr Carson, with a view to bringing up the numbers, was that Greek should no longer be compulsory in his class; but the Council would have none of this revolutionary proposal. A suggestion made in the following year for the introduction of Natural Science was supported by Mackay, Pyper and Boyd, but strongly opposed by Carson and the former Rector, Pillans, now Professor in the University; so it was allowed to drop. In the same year Carson got his way about Greek, and it was made optional in the Rector's class.

The important matter of holidays came to the

front in 1839, when the Council refused to grant a petition from the pupils praying them to suspend for the future the meetings of the School on Saturdays. In the same year the course of study was again revised, the principal alterations being that the study of Greek in the Third Class was postponed till March, while Higher Arithmetic and Algebra were added to the work of the Rector's class, which also got Geometry and Algebra from three to four, and Practical Mathematics from eight to nine. It was stipulated that the last-mentioned subject should begin on 1st April, surely an inappropriate date for a practical subject. This system of enlarging the curriculum by means of classes before or after the regular hours can hardly have been popular with the pupils, but it clearly represents a desire to make the best of both worlds—to find room for the modern subjects, without which the numbers were likely to decrease, and at the same time to maintain the full vigour of the classical training which was the traditional mainstay of the School.

In 1843 an additional subject, which was probably more acceptable to the pupils, was introduced, when Mr Roland obtained permission to teach fencing " at hours when boys are disengaged." Two years later, German made its first appearance, a few months before Dr Schmitz became Rector.

Natural Science, repulsed in 1836, returned to the attack and forced an entrance in 1848. On this occasion " the Rector and other Classical Masters were unanimous in approving the introduction." Carson, of course, had given place to Schmitz, which explains the change of attitude. Natural History and Chemistry were the branches selected.

From the minute dealing with this matter we get casually the information that the normal hours on Saturday are from nine to eleven, so the day of deliverance is drawing nearer. It comes in 1851, when the College Committee report that " on various grounds unnecessary to be detailed, but principally in consideration of the severe and trying nature of their studies during the other five days of the week, and with a due regard to the health and reasonable recreation of the boys, the Committee unanimously recommend that, with the exception of Gymnastics, all teaching in the School should be suspended on the Saturdays; but that, with a view to compensating so far for this indulgence to both Teachers and Pupils, the quarter days should cease to be holidays as heretofore." Admirable sentiments admirably expressed.

The same Committee make further progress in broadening the curriculum. Beginning with the customary profession of faith: " The Committee think it right to state at the outset that in all their deliberations they have kept steadily in view the maintenance of the high character of the School as a classical seminary, and they feel satisfied that this can be done and at the same time additional opportunities afforded to the pupils for the acquisition of other branches of knowledge of a more practical character and better suited to the views and prospects of those who have no intention of following any of the learned professions," they proceed to recommend that the hours of classical study be reduced from five to four daily. " This important alteration," they say, " goes to the root of most of the other alterations of the curriculum "; but " the learned and eminent Rector," Dr Schmitz, assures them that " the classical or learned character of the School can be maintained without any loss of efficiency." They then proceed to make it clear that no boy need take Greek if he does not wish to do so. Under the erroneous impression that Greek was compulsory, " many boys not destined for the liberal professions are removed in the third and fourth years from a desire on the part of the parents to give to their education more of a commercial character, and the idea that this could not be obtained in the High School owing to Greek being compulsory." They point out that this is an entire mistake, and that the time-table " has been so framed that the class of boy referred to may continue to attend for Latin and English, and at the same time devote the hour employed by their fellows in learning Greek to attendance on such subsidiary branches as may be best suited to the tastes and future prospects of the boys." They even go so far as to consider and at one time approve the appointment of a separate English master, but finally reject the idea, and this reform has to wait. " It will readily occur to every Member of Council," they conclude, " that our Educational Institutions cannot stand still—they must be progressive." The upholders of the strict classical tradition had put up a good fight, worthy of the Romans who were their spiritual ancestors, and it is all to their credit that ultimately, if somewhat reluctantly, they moved with the times, or, at least, a little after them.

Subsequent changes in the curriculum, though both numerous and important, are of less historic interest, for the battle has now been fought and lost, or won, according to the point of view. The optional subjects

which have hitherto hung about the fringes of
the time-table are now admitted to an equality
of status, though not yet of time. All that
follows follows naturally and inevitably. There
is no standing still. And it is only right that
full acknowledgment should be made of the
services rendered to the cause of educational
progress by " the learned and eminent Rector,"
Dr Leonhard Schmitz. No one can go through
the contemporary documents without realising
how liberal and enlightened were his views,
and how fully he was trusted by the Town
Council. A graduate of Bonn, the University
of the Prince Consort, he may have owed something to that connection. But his talents were
his own, and whatever the source of his
authority, he used it wisely and with marked
benefit to the School. His predecessor, Carson,
was the last and by no means the least of a
long line of distinguished Rectors in the old
tradition. Schmitz, himself a distinguished
classical scholar, was the first in the new, and
the choice proved a happy one.

Perhaps the most outstanding development
of the last fifty years has been the increasing
attention paid to organised athletics. It is a
little curious that those who were so devoted
to the classical tradition paid hardly any attention to the familiar saying, " *Mens sana in*

corpore sano." As far back, it is true, as 1610 the Treasurer was ordained " to cause big ane pair of Butts to the scholaris of Hie School beside the same at the tounis wall "; and we have already noted the introduction of a fencing class. But the real beginning of Athletics dates from the end of 1859, when an application was made by Lord Provost Melville to the Board of Works for permission for the boys of the High School " to play at cricket in Holyrood Park." In his letter the Lord Provost states that he is writing " at the request of Dr Schmitz, the eminent Rector of the School." When we remember that in 1859 H.R.H. the Prince of Wales was in residence at Holyrood, and was a pupil of Dr Schmitz, we can surmise whose influence induced Her Majesty's First Commissioner of Works in 1860 to grant a favourable answer to the application. In this way we obtained the tenancy of our first athletic field, which we still retain.

Now that we have set Athletics in their rightful place in the School Curriculum, it will be more convenient to complete our survey of the purely academic changes, and subsequently to trace athletic development. On the former side the record is mainly one of adjustment of balance. Subject after subject gains recognition, and each introduction necessarily involves some diminution in the time allotted to other subjects. The Classics, starting with the lion's share, have inevitably to make the largest concessions. When Dr Schmitz retired in 1865, a Committee was appointed to overhaul the whole system. This was a very full inquiry, and a decision was not reached till well on in the next year. How perplexing some at least of the Councillors found their task may be gathered from the fact that Bailie Lewis solemnly proposed " to farm out the buildings of the High School to a properly qualified party "; but he got only one supporter. Ultimately the following scheme of re-organisation was adopted, prefaced by the customary confession of faith. " Their aim is to increase the efficiency of the Classical Department by making it quite distinct and separate from the others; to do the same for English by giving it a position co-ordinate with the Classical masters." Accordingly they recommend the recognition of five Departments: Classics (where efficiency is to be promoted by reducing the staff from five to three); English; Foreign Languages; Mathematics and Arithmetic; Miscellaneous (including Writing, Drawing, Fencing, Physical Science, and a Civil Service Class). While pupils were encouraged to follow a prescribed course, Classics and English alone were obligatory; elsewhere options were allowed with the Rector's sanction.

At this stage the High School Club makes, so far as we know, its first intervention in the affairs of the School. A deputation headed by that stout warrior, Bailie Colston, makes a vigorous protest against reform. The reasons, given at great length and with singular animation, range from an Act of Council in 1654 to " the all but universal testimony of the most eminent educationists in Scotland." But the worthy Bailie's eloquence fell on deaf ears and the reforms were put into execution. Indeed they were carried further. Dr John Merry Ross and Mr David Munn were appointed English and Mathematics masters respectively. Arithmetic was separated from Mathematics, and, finally, Lieutenant Mackie was added to the Staff as Teacher of Fortification. But the divorce between Arithmetic and Mathematics was annulled in the following year, when the Arithmetic master, Mr Moffat, retired.

This constitution of the curriculum continued till the year 1873, when a definite modern course was introduced. " Formerly," says Dr Donaldson, in his Rector's Report, " we had fallen into an attempt to supply a kind of education not exactly adapted for those who go to the Universities nor for those who go to business, but a sort of compromise between them. . . . We are now to make the effort to give a thorough modern education, and we are to strive to make those boys who take the modern side work with all the earnestness and devotion which have distinguished the classical." A further step in this direction was taken in 1885, when a Sixth Commercial Class was formed; in subsequent years this was expanded into a complete Commercial Course. The completion of the Gymnasium and Swimming Bath in the same year brought these subjects within the regular curriculum. Hitherto the one had been an extra and the other non-existent. Looking to the views of Ancient Greece, we should perhaps regard this change as a reversion to the classical tradition rather than as a modern innovation. At the same time the system of Honours Certificates for those immediately outside the Prize List was instituted. During the first World War all prizes except the endowed Medals and Prizes were abolished, and these Honours Certificates took their place.

The next important change was the introduction of the Preparatory Department in 1887. Up to this time the boys had come to the School about the age of nine, their previous education being obtained in one or other of the numerous private preparatory schools which existed in the city. Dr Marshall, in his Rector's Report, gives the following reason for the new departure: " We have found by experience that every year the preparatory schools which have been in the habit of supplying us with a considerable portion of our pupils have been extending their curriculum upwards, till now some of them profess to prepare for the Universities. Under these circumstances our first class more especially has suffered serious diminution, and the pupils when they first come to us, not having been trained on a plan identical with ours, are not fitted to join our work with the same success as they would have been had we trained them from the first." Dr Marshall's original idea was to have several preparatory schools, one in each residential quarter of the town, and so obviate the difficulties of transport for young boys, but this plan was not adopted, and the original preparatory classes were housed in the same buildings as the rest of the School. From the outset the new Department was an unqualified success, due in no small measure to the happy choice of its first teachers, Miss Home and Miss Findlay, and of Miss Maclaren, who joined them a few years later.

At the same time, as a further development of the Modern and Commercial sides, a chemical laboratory was fitted up, and this policy was extended four years later when a physics laboratory and workshop were opened. These piecemeal developments were at first housed in somewhat makeshift abodes, but eventually the authorities, convinced that these things had come to stay and were going to grow, faced the problem and added to the buildings at the north-east end of the playground. This extension was completed in 1895. In the same year a School Choir was instituted. This was a voluntary body, which did its work after school hours, conducted by Mr Fitzgerald, whose official status was that of assistant in the Commercial Department. It was not till 1908 that an official Singing Master —Mr Stronach—was appointed. Other subjects received additional recognition in 1908, when " the greatly enlarged scope of teaching in Science and in Drawing made it imperative to secure the continuous and exclusive services of specially appointed masters in these two Departments." For thirty-three, twenty-two and fifteen years respectively, Dr Andrew Wilson (Physics), Dr Drinkwater (Chemistry), and Mr Reid (Drawing) had given with much acceptance part-time instruction in their

LEONHARD
SCHMITZ,
Ph.D., LL.D.
1845 - 1865

JAMES
DONALDSON,
M.A., LL.D.
1866 - 1882

JOHN MARSHALL
M.A., LL.D.
1882 - 1909

RECTORS

subjects. Now Mr J. G. Lindsay was appointed Science Master and Mr R. S. McIntosh Art Master. In addition to the work of their Departments the services of Mr Lindsay to Football and Mr McIntosh to the O.T.C., of which he was the first commandant, were highly appreciated.

In 1909 there was a further re-organisation. History and Geography were separated from English—two members of the staff, Mr Muir and Mr Ross, being appointed Geography and History masters respectively. With a view to the better classification of the boys in their respective classes, the old nomenclature of Classical, Modern, and Commercial was abandoned, and the terms A and B (in some cases Senior and Junior) Divisions were adopted. A Divisions took Latin, B did not. When, later, C Divisions were added, both A and B Divisions took Latin, C did not. As between A and B, A took Greek, B did not. This system of classification purely by linguistic tests was not wholly satisfactory, and led to subsequent modifications within these Divisions.

A further change of nomenclature took place in 1920. The development of the Preparatory and Junior schools had led to numerical confusion. As a way out of the difficulty the term " class " was confined to these two schools, and the term " Form " applied to the Senior school. This gave four Preparatory and three Junior school classes, with or without Divisions, as numbers required, and six Forms in A, B, and generally C Divisions. There are now seven double classes or stages in what has come to be known as the " Prep " School, and six Forms, suitably divided, in the Senior School.

One innovation allied to the curriculum finds its place here. Under our present Rector, Dr Imrie, the liason between Rector and Staff on the one hand and parents on the other is being developed to the advantage of both parties and to the benefit of the most important member of the School community, the pupil.

Since that day in 1595 when William Sinclair shot Bailie John MacMorane there is ample evidence through the ages that the boys of the School were not deficient in martial ardour, and spasmodic attempts were made to guide it along wiser and safer paths, the first being the erection of shooting butts in 1610. At various times we get traces that instruction in drill is given by janitors, and even, in 1865, that the Town Council authorised the provision of 100 constabulary carbines, including bayonets and scabbards, at a cost of about 7s. 6d. apiece, " in order that the boys may learn the Manual and Platoon Exercises, and Bayonet and Position Drill." The price suggests that the carbines were condemned ones. Did some dim promptings of memory warn the City Fathers that a dummy shotgun might be safer? And we have heard of our Fencing Master and our Teacher of Fortification. In 1926, after long years of waiting, these intermittent incursions into the field of Mars were replaced by the Officers' Training Corps which has proved one of the most popular and also one of the most valuable educative forces in the School. In 1940 Officers' Training Corps were renamed Junior Training Corps. In 1941 Air Training Corps were instituted and the School immediately responded by raising a contingent. In 1948 the powers that be introduced a new scheme whereby the two forces were linked under the title of Combined Cadet Force. There for the moment the matter stands.

It is natural that in recent years the changes should have been, or should seem to have been more frequent. Apart from the fact that our information is fuller, the multiplicity of new subjects and new ideas—sometimes old ones resurrected—has made that inevitable. It may be that some of the changes were productive

of " muckle cry and little oo," but others have
had a marked influence. The widening of the
scope and meaning of education in the school
community seen in such extra-mural or extra-
class-room activities as *Schola Regia*, the
Literary and Debating Society, the Photo-
graphic Society, school concerts, plays, Scouts
and camps have all made for a fuller life.
If the curriculum has lost something in depth,
it has gained in breadth. To one who has
watched the process for longer than he cares
to recall the most notable developments have
been in the realms of Art, of Music, of the
Drama, and of Athletics—all of them surely
in the best tradition of Ancient Greece.

And now we may briefly trace the development of organised athletics. That Act of
Council in 1851, which freed our Saturdays,
should be held in high esteem by all our
athletes, for it is the Magna Carta of our
Cricket and Football Clubs. It rendered possible the formation of a Cricket Club in 1861,
to be followed seven years later by a Football
Club. In the early days former and present
pupils seem to have played together, and the
date of separation is not recorded. The School
Games also date from the early 'sixties. Unlike
Cricket and Football these latter appear to have
been organised by the masters. We hesitate to

suggest that the masters of to-day are in any way comparable to the giants of the past, but it is a fact that these ancient worthies found this burden too heavy for them. At Dr Donaldson's request the work was undertaken by the Former Pupils' Cricket Club, which successfully carried on its task up to the outbreak of the War.

In the earlier stages then, Cricket and Football were organised by the boys themselves, with valuable, if intermittent help from enthusiastic former pupils. An older generation will remember with affection the work of men like Taverner Knott and Nat Watt in this connection. Nor can we omit to recall the unofficial but no less welcome encouragement of Mr Thomson Whyte, perhaps the first of our masters who took a keen interest in School sport. The change began in 1900 when, at the request of the respective Captains of Cricket and Football, two of the masters undertook the management of these sports. The experiment proved successful and was extended when, in 1912, the " Nation " system was introduced. Under this system all boys on coming to School are allotted to one of four " Nations," and competitions, both in Athletics and in Scholarship, are held annually to decide which is the champion Nation. The introduction of Scholarship we owe to Dr W. J.

Watson, the Rector at this date, who held strongly the view that all boys, and not merely those at the top, should be given an incentive to pull their weight on the academic side. He was anxious to see the team spirit enter into work as well as into play. At the same time the masters were similarly allotted to the various Nations, and were also divided up into committees responsible for assisting the various external activities. The formation of these committees made it possible in Cricket and Football to help boys at various stages, instead of confining the work practically to the First XI. and XV., and in this way to develop " Under 15 " and " Under 13 " teams. The great growth in the number of teams is the best evidence that the system is a satisfactory one. We have seen how the School hours have shrunk through the ages. The converse is true as regards the hours of the Staff.

So in many ways the curriculum, in the widest sense, has changed. New subjects and new methods have modified the old, for " our Educational Institutions cannot stand still— they must be progressive." But with it all the ancient tradition persists. Whatever the method, the aim is still what it was in the days of Hercules Rollock, " to instruct the youth in pietie, guid maneris, doctrine and letteris."

CLUBS OF THE SCHOOL

AN attempt to sketch the history of High School
Clubs recalls the tribulations of the Hebrews.
The straw, indeed, is not wholly wanting, but
it is sadly deficient in quantity. A cash book,
valuable and at times illuminating, is but
scanty material for the historian; but it is
milk and honey compared with an album of
photographs depicting respectable early Vic-
torian gentlemen complete with tall hats, frock
coats and voluminous whiskers, which forms the
sole surviving memorial of the Irvine Club.
And yet a Club which numbered among its
members Horatius Bonar, James Nasmyth and
Robert Reid, " dentist to the Queen," is not a
Club to be forgotten. Enough at least remains
to give a picture of a phase of School life—the
Class Club—which the altered circumstances of
the curriculum have rendered a thing of the
past, though the modern " Form " Club may
perhaps claim a spiritual affinity.

Pride of place, however, must be given to the
Royal High School Club, not the oldest, but
certainly the most important of our clubs. The
present Club is not the first to bear the title of

High School (changed in 1907 to Royal High School) Club. In 1808 fourteen former pupils banded themselves together and commissioned Raeburn to paint a portrait of Dr Adam. They must have maintained some form of association, as in subsequent legal proceedings with regard to that portrait they figure as " The High School Club." When, in 1859, they remove the portrait and hand it over to the Scottish National Gallery, Mr John Cockburn writes: " It being the intention of the surviving members (five in number) of the High School Club," etc. All they seem to have done for the School, however, was to persuade Dr Adam to sit for his portrait under the belief, according to his son, that it would remain a permanent possession of the School to which he gave his life, and then to deprive the School of that possession. This action indicates a feeling of which we get traces also in the Class Clubs. The loyalties of pupils in those days were particular rather than general. They were fellow pupils in the class of Adam, or Irvine, or Boyd, more than they were old boys of the High School. The system whereby a boy spent four years with one master, and frequently two with the Rector—and practically all his day at that—quite naturally fostered this feeling.

When the present Club was founded in 1849,

Dr Schmitz had been Rector for four years and the process of breaking down the old four-master tradition was on the way. There were still Class Clubs to come, but their heyday was over, and the wider conception of membership of a great corporate body was gaining ground. The Secretary of the preliminary committee, the first person to be entered in the cash book of the Club, is very appropriately Dr Steven, the first historian of the School.

The first Annual Report, dated July 1850, containing the original constitution, has fortunately been preserved, and so have the Accounts from the beginning. From these we learn that the first President was the Earl of Camperdown. On his death he was succeeded by Lord Brougham. The Club grew and accumulated funds, but presently it met with a serious reverse. The auditor's docket for 1857 states that " there is a balance of two hundred and twenty nine pounds and one shilling remaining in the hands of Mr ——, which cannot at present be recovered from him." It is not till 1878 that " a dividend of four shillings and fourpence in the pound on the estate of the late Mr —— yields the sum of forty-nine pounds twelve shillings and sevenpence." This matter would have been left in oblivion but for two things. It brought about a change in the subscription. Previously the only entry is one guinea. In 1858 we meet with the first entry of ten shillings and sixpence, the sum now paid by one who joins within a year of leaving School. And from December 1857 we meet with a number of entries with the word " repetition " annexed. The members faced their troubles manfully, and in many cases voluntarily paid their subscriptions over again to set the Club on its feet; a very practical exhibition of their interest in the School.

With this generous support the Club soon recovered from its difficulties, and in 1862 we note the first record of an investment: one hundred pounds debenture stock of the Scottish Central Railway. The subsequent financial history of the Club is one of steady and uneventful progress. When we recollect that the Treasurers were men like Mark Sanderson and the late James Aikman Smith, the latter of whom held office for forty years, this is not surprising. True, a stray Report of the Committee, dated 1888, which has been preserved, makes mention of the number of members who have joined " since the reconstruction." But what this reconstruction was and why it took place is " wrop in mystery." The cash book shows no evidence of any intermission in the Club's functioning, and we must conclude that the matter was not a serious one.

The growth of membership has some interesting features. At December 1850, the end of the first full year, it stood at 247. Fifty years later the total enrolment numbered 829, an addition of 582 names. Another twenty years saw 178 additions, while the twelve years from 1921 to 1932 added 562 names to the roll. This striking increase was undoubtedly due to the energy with which the Rector, Dr King Gillies, put the claims of the Club before boys leaving School. In the twelve years 1901 to 1912 the number of boys who joined on leaving School was 30. In the years 1921 to 1932 the number was 415. This is clear evidence that the liaison between the Club and the School has been greatly strengthened, and that the Club has taken an established place as one of the essential institutions of the School. It is further evidence of the activity of the Club that the number of those joining some years after leaving School has also gone up. In the former period the number was 69, in the latter 147, and for this the credit goes to the energetic Secretaries, A. A. Gibb, J. W. Loudon, J. Gill and E. W. Wilson and the Treasurers, James Aikman Smith and Stephen Kerr. The Club has been equally fortunate in its other office-bearers. Successive Presidents, from Camperdown and Brougham down to the Very Reverend Principal Sir George Adam Smith, a great-grand-nephew of the famous Rector, Alexander Adam, and the present President, Sir Francis J. Grant, K.C.V.O., LL.D., W.S., Emeritus Lord Lyon King of Arms, have rendered yeoman service ably supported by their Vice-Presidents, officials and members of Committee. The flourishing condition of the Club is the best tribute to their ungrudging labours.

In 1939, when he retired from the office of President, Sir George Adam Smith was elected the first Honorary President of the Club, a well-deserved tribute to his long and deep interest in its welfare. In the following year a similar and equally well-deserved tribute was paid to Dr William King Gillies who, in his twenty-one years as Rector, had done much to strengthen the bonds between Present and Former Pupils.

" The objects of the Club shall be generally to promote the interests of the High School, maintain a good understanding, and form a bond of union among the Former Pupils of that institution." So runs Clause IV. of the Constitution, and the Club has sedulously and with a wise discretion pursued these objects. Apart from the Club Prize, the funds for which

in early days were collected at the Annual
General Meeting, it has given since 1863 an
annual prize at the School Games.   Since 1886
it has aided the School Magazine by an
advertisement, the rate of payment for which
is not calculated on commercial lines.   It has
spent considerable sums on the purchase and
framing of engravings of distinguished former
pupils which now adorn the walls of the School.
It gave a grant towards the production of the
first Roll of Honour and has similarly assisted
the second.   When the memorial stone to Dr
Adam in Buccleuch Parish churchyard had
fallen into disrepair, it was the Club that
raised the funds to have the necessary repairs
executed.   In these and in other ways it has
shown an unostentatious but practical interest
in the welfare of the School, with the result that
it has become the natural trustee of various
funds raised by former pupils to commemorate
individuals connected with the School.   It
administers the funds of the Carson Medal,
India Prize, Carmichael Medal, Inches Prize,
Chisholm Prize, Bruce Prize, Norman Howard
Small Memorial Prize, and Muir Memorial
Medal.   It gives the R.H.S. Club Prize to
the Dux of the School.   It also provides the
funds for the John Marshall and Scott Centenary Medals, and has recently presented the

James Aikman Smith Cup. It has given encouragement to the foundation of Royal High School Clubs furth of Scotland, and has perhaps reaped the benefit in a well-deserved increase in its own membership.

When the interests of the School have in any way been menaced it has been active in their defence, a notable instance being the proposed conversion, in 1904, of the School into an Art Gallery. The report prepared for the Club by Mr Henry F. Kerr, A.R.I.B.A., aroused so much opposition to this wild-cat scheme that it was discreetly shelved.

But the officials of the Club believe that the old saying " all work and no play makes Jack a dull boy " is as applicable to old boys as to the young. The annual luncheons and dinners of the Club " maintain a good understanding and form a bond of union among the Former Pupils." They give the opportunity of meeting old classmates, of recalling old memories, mellowed and magnified it may be by the mists of time, and of keeping alive that spirit of " the old School " which it is the true function of a Former Pupils' Club to foster.

.   .   .   .   .

Turning now to the Class Clubs we have been able to trace the existence of several, the details being given at the end of this section

(p. 101). The Rector's Report of 1878, which gives a list of " the more recent Clubs," states that " there are several older Clubs in regard to which I should have wished to have given information." So should I, but the information is not available. Some of them are little more than names, and the evidence for their existence is contained in Annual Reports which testify that they presented prizes, or in *Schola Regia*, where occasional meetings are recorded. But their minute books, if any, have disappeared from view, buried perhaps in that great repository of other people's property, the dusty attic of a lawyer's office. We know, for instance, that a band of Pillans' old boys combined to have his portrait painted by Raeburn, and presented it to the School. As this was in 1827 it is incredible that they did not meet and have a dinner with a suitably lengthy toast list on this auspicious occasion. But no record of it or of any subsequent gathering survives. Similarly, Dr Carson's old boys had his portrait painted by Mr (afterwards Sir John) Watson Gordon, and presented to the School in 1833. They, too, must have dined and wined. Indeed, the Report of 1878 refers to Pillans and Carson Clubs as among the lost legions. Again, *Schola Regia*, in 1897, records a dinner of the 1865-71 Class, which appears to have been a Carmichael Class. From Dr Colston's *History of Dr Boyd's Fourth High School Class Club* we can infer that previous Boyd Classes had also formed Clubs, and we also get the interesting information that in the Crimea there were two Boyd Clubs formed by officers, obviously in different quadrennia: for the true Class Club man resembled the Jews; he would have no dealings with the Samaritans of other periods than his own. In the second Mackay Class Club minutes it is solemnly recorded that three gentlemen on the original roll of the class have "forfeited their right of membership." It was a rule of this club that anyone who had attended at any time the class of any other classical master was not a Mackay (1820-23) pupil *pur sang*, and these three unfortunates had the bar sinister of Pyper on their escutcheons.

The later Clubs were not strictly Class Clubs in this puritanical sense, but for convenience we have grouped together under one heading the Class Club proper and the later " Classes " Club open to all pupils of a particular master, whatever their years of attendance. In his *History of Dr Boyd's Fourth Class Club*, Colston animadverts with sorrow on this change. Speaking of the Macmillan Club, he says: " I cannot help here expressing regret that

WILLIAM JOHN
WATSON, M.A., LL.D.
1909 - 1914

JOHN STRONG
C.B.E., M.A., LL.D.
1914 - 1919

WILLIAM KING
GILLIES, M.A., LL.D.
1919 ---- 1940

RECTORS

in place of the Class Clubs which were previously formed, Clubs in honour of the master who taught them have been substituted. Mr Macmillan's pupils were the innovators, and they have been succeeded by those of Drs Donaldson and Bryce and the late Mr John Carmichael. . . . With the pupils of Dr Boyd, High School Class Clubs are apparently to end. This is a notable falling away in the *esprit de corps* of High School Boys of former days." Colston's idea was that the essence of these Clubs was fellowship at School. It is quite a reasonable view, but there was surely room for both types. As a matter of fact, Class Clubs were still to come into existence, but the change which Colston laments was merely a step in the new direction. It may be that the whirligig of time will bring in his revenges. The Class or Classes Club passed away as the system of teaching, with its growing variety of subjects, spread the time of boys over a number of masters. The recent development of the Form system, whereby a Form during practically all its years is under the particular charge of one master, has partially restored the old idea, and provided the necessary link. Recently one Form, some years after leaving School, united to present a trophy for inter-Form competition in athletics, which has done much to stimulate the corporate spirit of the Form without impairing the larger loyalties. Perhaps the future may see the growth of Form Clubs as nebulae in the universe of the Royal High School Club. I respectfully dedicate this propitiatory idea to the *manes* of Bailie Colston.

These Class Clubs were all, as one secretary phrases it, " convivial " clubs. Their main purpose was an annual meeting for the recalling of old times; a lengthy process in some cases, if we may judge from the minutes of the Mackay Class (1820-23) Club. From these it appears that the members not infrequently met for dinner and stayed on to supper. As the Class had an enrolment of 288, doubtless it took the twenty or so members who met some time to cover the ground. Again, at the first meeting of Dr Boyd's Fourth Class Club there was a toast list of twenty-three items, fourteen of which called for replies. As there were only twenty-five members present, many of them had to work a double shift. Small wonder that the dinners of those days began at the early hour of 5.30, or that members required to sustain themselves with supper later on. As time goes on the fashion of lengthy toast lists passes away; the gatherings become too small to cope with them, and more inclined to reminiscence, as witness the minute of Dr Boyd's Fifth Class Club for March 1886: "After a lapse of many years the following (eight in number) old Class fellows met in the Waterloo Hotel, where they dined and enjoyed a pleasant evening talking together of their school days and school companions, telling anecdotes, singing songs, and thinking they were boys again."

Naturally, famous names are to be found in Class lists covering so wide a period. One unique distinction which falls to the lot of the earlier Mackay Club may be cited. Among its active members were two who held concurrently the two highest positions in our Scottish legal hierarchy—Lord Justice-General Inglis and Lord Justice-Clerk Moncrieff. This would have rejoiced the heart of old Benjamin Mackay who had a flair for by-ordinar things.

The natural termination of all these Clubs is obvious. Such minute books as survive tell the same tale—a diminishing attendance and finally a blank. There is a pathetic note in the last entry in the minute book of Dr Boyd's Fifth Class Club: " On the invitation of their old classfellow, William Mackie, John Sommerville, J. Murray Thomson and James Murdoch met at the house of the first-mentioned on the evening of Friday, 30th November (1908-9 or -10), to have a chat about their schooldays more than fifty years ago. The four above named are all dead now but myself, and I have only to say that all the instructions given at the last meetings of the class-fellows were carried out. J. M., 9th March 1912."

And here is the only written trace of the Irvine Club that I have discovered. In a pamphlet preserved in the Public Library, Mr K. C. Whyte tells us that Lord Provost Adam Black was a member of the Irvine Class Club. " This Club," he says, " ran its course as few Clubs have done. Year after year the table got shorter and the death-roll longer, until one day Mr Black got a note from Claud Muirhead, the Secretary, intimating that the dinner day was that day fortnight; that they two were all that remained; and that the dinner would require to be held at Mr Muirhead's bedside, for he was quite confined to bed. The Club did dine. They took affectionate leave of each other, and within a fortnight the Club, in the person of Mr Black, attended the Secretary's funeral."

.   .   .   .   .

Of all our Clubs to-day, perhaps the most widely known, because they are literally the most active, are the various Sports Clubs connected with the School. Of these the oldest is the Cricket Club, founded in 1861. The original meeting was held in a sentry-box in Holyrood Park, which must have been a tight fit for the three stout-hearted gentlemen who attended and duly elected themselves to the respective offices of Captain, Secretary and Treasurer. Perhaps the Treasurer had to stand outside. For the next four years this sentry-box, *mirabile dictu*, did duty as a pavilion. From these small beginnings the Club steadily grew. It raised the money to build first one and then, in 1879, a second and more spacious pavilion, designed by a Former Pupil; to level the field and enclose it (1877-8) with the present railing. In 1897, to cope with the growth of Athletics at School, it took a lease of Corstorphine Field, formerly tenanted by the University. Here it was joined by the Football Club as sub-tenants. This Club had been started in 1868 and at first played at Holyrood. Subsequently it had several migrations. Raimes Park (Bonnington), Warrender Park, Blantyre Terrace, Grange Loan and Newington all housed it from time to time till it joined the Cricket Club at Corstorphine.

This migration of the two Clubs, and the cause of it, made the financial question acute. So it was accompanied by a Bazaar, which raised a net sum of £1740 10s. 11d. This, after meeting some much-needed capital ex-

penditure on the pavilion at Holyrood, wa
vested in Trustees and the interest used t
assist the Cricket and Football Clubs in thei
work of carrying on the School athletics. O
the formation of the Athletic Club the balance
with the consent of the Former Pupils' Cricke
and Football Clubs, was handed over to th
War Memorial Fund.

The War interrupted the activities of bot
Clubs, while those of the School were perforc
carried on. Even before the War it was felt tha
responsibility for the School Athletics, whic
on the financial side fell mainly on the Forme
Pupils' Cricket Club, was too heavy a burde
for a small body with no resources behind it
No less than three attempts had been made t
form an Athletic Club, all of them unsuccessful
But the War forced everybody's hands. Grea
credit is due to the Former Pupils' Cricket Clul
for long years of hard and often anxious work,
without which School Athletics would probably
have gone to the wall. The burden had beer
torn from their shoulders in the convulsion o
1914. It was impossible, even had they been
willing, that they should attempt to resume it in
the altered circumstances of 1919. Clearly the
attempt which had thrice failed would have to
be made again. This time it was successfu
and on a larger scale, for it included the present

as well as the former pupils. Partly this result was due to the force of circumstances overcoming the natural reluctance of the Former Pupils' Clubs to the apparent loss of a long and distinguished individual existence. But a large share of the credit for bringing the negotiations to a successful issue was due to the Rector, Dr W. King Gillies. By raising the Athletic Fee at School, and by securing more liberal support from the Education Authority, he made it possible for the present pupils to become equal partners, bearing their fair share of the burden. The upshot was the formation of an Athletic Club, embracing both former and present pupils, and undertaking the financial responsibility for ground and general management, while leaving to the individual sections the management of their own particular affairs. At the same time the Memorial Field at Jock's Lodge was acquired and the tenancy of Corstorphine was given up. The original branches of the Club were the Present and Former Pupils' Cricket and Football Sections. With the development of track and field athletics two new sections were added in 1949. Present and Former Pupils' Athletic Sections. The headquarters of these sections is at Holyrood, where it is proposed in future to hold the School Annual Games.

This is not the place for attempting a histor
of the doings of either Club on the field. Suc
records as are available will be found at th
end of the volume. But we may here note tha
the Football Club is an original member c
the Scottish Rugby Union; and it is fittin
to recall the great services rendered to th
administrative side of the game and to th
cause of genuine amateurism by the late Jame
Aikman Smith.

The Golf Club was formed in 1884. Ther
is mention of a Present Pupils' Golf Club i
1876. This was perhaps the nucleus from
which the Former Pupils' Club sprang; but
curiously enough, the circular calling th
meeting was issued by the Secretary of th
F.P. Cricket Club, and the names of thos
present have a familiar Cricket and Footba
ring. The Club started with a membership c
seventy-two, which included five Sanderson
Since then it has pursued its pleasant an
uneventful way, and still forms a link betwee
those who play and those who have played th
more active games.

· · · · ·

We come now to those Clubs which have bee
formed furth of Scotland. The earliest of thes
was the R.H.S. (London) Club, formed i
1889, its first President being Sir Theodor

Martin, and its Secretary Mr Herbert Toomer. After meeting for several years it fell into abeyance, but was revived mainly by the efforts of two former pupils in London, E. G. Laing and John Allan, and of J. J. Trotter at this end. The first President of the revived Club was Sir Archibald Geikie. During the War it was again in abeyance, but started to function once more in 1920, since when it has been in full vigour. In the years in which the Scotland-England Rugby International is played at Twickenham the Club holds its Annual Dinner on the Friday preceding the match. This affords an opportunity for former pupils from other parts meeting their old schoolfellows in the London area. The Club also presents annual prizes to the School. John Allan has been Secretary since the Club was revived.

The R.H.S. (Canada) Club was founded in 1913, and owed its existence chiefly to Donald Ross in Canada and to J. J. Trotter. The latter indeed was keenly interested in this side of the School life, and despite the Laodicean attitude of some of the older members of the Parent Club, who gloomily recalled the fate of the first London Club, persevered in his useful spade work and reaped his reward. The Canada Club had a brief but vigorous existence, during which it presented a " Canada Cup," which was won outright, and so is no longer with us. But the first World War put an end to its activities. In 1939 its place was to some extent filled by the formation of the R.H.S. Club at British Columbia.

The R.H.S. (India) Club is a more recent creation, having been started in 1925 " to promote the interests of the School, maintain a good understanding and form a bond of union among pupils in India and the East, and to welcome and take an interest in young Former Pupils coming to these parts for the first time." How efficiently it performs this last function is well known to those of us who have charge of the Former Pupils' Record Cards. T. J. Christie has been President since its inception, and its Secretaries have been H. A. Taylor, C. F. Henry and G. S. Young. In 1928 it presented the India Trophy to the School O.T.C., and in 1939 it gave the leopard skin and silver baton and staff. Looking to the long and honourable connection of the School with India, it is perhaps not surprising that the Club there, like the Club in London, the Scotsman's second home, should be in vigorous health.

Between the wars there was a flourishing Club in Malaya. The ravages of war dealt hardly with those out East, and post-war uncertainties have so far prevented a reconstruction.

Difficulties of distance and of numbers make the existence of formal Clubs in other parts of the Empire harder to maintain. But informal gatherings are held from time to time in many parts, which serve the purpose although they do not attain to the status of Clubs. And the existence in the School of a record of all former pupils known to be abroad ensures that wherever they go young former pupils will not be wholly without that helping hand which the London and India Clubs so readily and efficiently extend to those who come within their orbit.

.   .   .   .   .

The possibility suggested in 1934 (p. 90) has now become a reality and we give below a list of Form Clubs. These modern Form Clubs spring from the fact that each Form has a Form Master who, though by no means the sole teacher of the Form, is responsible for its various activities and so comes to be specially associated with its members. The war years have made it difficult for these clubs to function but many are resuming activity and we may expect others to be formed as time goes on. The date of foundation is given first. The

information in brackets indicates the membership qualification.

1934.	Bannerman	(1925-30).
1934.	Grant	(1928-33)
1936.	Hossack.	(IIIB 1935).
1936.	Thomsen.	(1934-35).
1937.	Dickson-Sandilands	(IVA 1934-35)
1937.	Baxter	(1932-37)
1937.	Burgoyne	(1934-35)
1938.	Bannerman	(1938)
1940.	Ross	(1940)
1941.	Law	(1937-38)
1941.	Dixon	(1936-42)
1941.	IV B/C 1939	(1935-41)
1943.	Mrs. Young	(Primary 5, 1942-43).

	I.	II.	Master.	Period of Service.
Pillans	? 1821	......	James Pillans, M.A.	R. 1810-20
Gray (1816-20) Class	1827	1877	James Gray, M.A.	1801-22
Irvine (1817-21) Class	? 1833 or 1857	......	George Irvine	1805-29
Carson	1833		Aglionby-Ross Carson, M.A., LL.D.	M. 1806-20
Mackay (1820-3) Class	1848	1891	Benjamin Mackay, M.A.	R. 1820-45
,, (1835-9) ,,	? 1867	1880	,, ,, ,,	1829-43
Pyper	1853	? 1875	William Pyper, M.A., LL.D.	1829-43
Boyd Fourth (1841-5) Class	1866	...	James Boyd, M.A., LL.D.	1822-44
,, Fifth (1848-9) ,,		1910	,, ,, ,,	1829-56
Carmichael (1865-71) Class		1897	John Carmichael ,, ,,	1829-56
Gunn			William Maxwell Gunn, M.A., LL.D.	1848-70
Macmillan	1863	1928	John Macmillan, M.A.	1843-51
Carmichael		...	John Carmichael	1844-66
Bryce		1888	Archibald Hamilton Bryce, M.A., LL.D.	1848-70
Donaldson	1873	...	James Donaldson, M.A., LL.D.	1852-67
Donaldson-Macdonald (1872-8) Class		1897	William Macdonald, M.A., LL.D.	M. 1856-66 / R. 1866-82
Donaldson-Jeffrey (1873-9) Class		1897	Thomson Jeffrey, M.A.	1866-77
,, (1875-81) Class		1897	,, ,, ,,	1871-82
1881-7 ,, Class				....
Marshall-Whyte Class	? 1910		John Marshall, M.A., LL.D.	R. 1882-1909
....			Thomson Whyte, M.A.	1883-1909

I. Gives date of foundation.

II. Gives date of last known meeting.

NOTE.—*The Caledonian Mercury*, February 1772, has advertisements of meetings of the members of the following classes. Whether they formed clubs or not is not known.

Mr. Gilchrist (1757-61), Mr. Bartlett (1756-62) and Mr. French (1759-63).

BENEFACTORS OF THE SCHOOL

First on the list of the benefactors of the School stands the name of the " Sair Sanct," David I.—not inappropriately in these days of economic stress, when men rail at the lavish expenditure on education. By his foundation of the Abbey of Holyrood, David, if he did not establish, at least endowed the School with sustenance. While his successors doubtless took an interest in the work, witness James V.'s charter confirming the Abbot of Holyrood's appointment of Henry Henryson as co-Rector and successor to David Vocat, I cannot find that they ever put their hands in their pockets to help it. Probably they felt that the Abbot of Holyrood was better able than they were to provide financial resources. But indirectly at least Mary of Gueldres, the widow of James II., did us a good turn, as we shall see later.

To Mary, Queen of Scots, we owe a part of our present income, and also our position as the " Town's School." The Reformation had given both Crown and nobility much of the property of the old Church, and part of what had gone to the Crown now came to the Town. In 1566, Mary vested the ecclesiastical patronages and endowments in Edinburgh in the Magistrates. These included the Grammar School, previously vested in the Abbot of Holyrood. In this way began the connection between the School and the Town Council, which has subsisted ever since.

Her son, James VI., the Scottish Solomon, is well known alike for his interest in learning and for his frugal mind. His contribution was fair words and the title *Schola Regia Edimburgensis*, a tribute both to his Latinity and to his parsimony. This was probably in 1590, when he made a state entry into Edinburgh with his newly-wed consort, Anne of Denmark, on which occasion Hercules Rollock, Rector of the School, delivered an oration of welcome " at the strait of the Bow " and also wrote a long Latin epithalamium which was much admired by the Royal pair.

Our next Royal benefaction was indirectly due to the greatest of our former pupils. In 1822 Sir Walter Scott had organised the visit of George IV. to Scotland. In 1825 the Royal visitor, on the suggestion of another distinguished former pupil, Viscount Melville, subscribed £500 to the fund for a new building for

Scott's old School. Since then the interest of
the Royal Family in the School has been
maintained. Queen Victoria sent her eldest
son for part of his education to the then Rector,
Dr Schmitz. In 1859 the Prince, afterwards
King Edward VII., presented the Carson Medal
on Prize Day. In 1925 his grandson, Prince
Henry, opened the Pavilion at the Memorial
Field, and graciously accepted Honorary Life
Membership of the Athletic Club.

.   .   .   .   .

There are traces of some early benefactions
of which little is now known. In 1616 the Kirk
Session of Edinburgh mortified the sum of
2000 merks in the City funds, the interest
thereof in all time coming to be divided among
" the four doctors of the Grammar School."
The Town lent the money to Harry Hope,
merchant, at 10 per cent., which he was to pay
to the said four doctors. He repaid the loan
in the next year to the City Treasurer, and that
is the last we hear of the money. Possibly it
has been merged in the Common Good. At
any rate, whoever now gets the interest, it
does not reach the apostolic successors of the
four doctors.

In 1639 Dr Robert Johnstone left a sum of
money, part of the interest of which was to be
divided yearly among four scholars of the High

JAMES JACKSON
ROBERTSON,
1940-1942

ALBERT HARRY
ROY BALL,
1942-1948

DAVID STUART
MELVILLE IMRIE,
1948----

RECTORS

School. Again there is no record of what became of this money.

In 1754 John Penman mortified the sum of £387 15s. 6d. for educational purposes. A portion of the interest amounting, after the extinction of a liferent, to £3 19s., was to be paid to a scholar to be educated at the High School of Edinburgh. The trustees were William Little Gilmour of Liberton and Craigmillar and his heirs, whom failing the Moderator of the Presbytery of Edinburgh for the time being and his successors in office. And that is all we hear of John Penman's Mortification. That these pious donors intended to benefit the School is clear. What is not so clear is whether their intentions were carried out. But we must, if somewhat literally, take the will for the deed and give them place as at least intending benefactors of the School.

While we do not seem to have had much luck with these early benefactions, we have come off better with the " Teinds in the Parishes of Sprouston, including Lempitlaw and Monimail." The story of these teinds takes us back to the founding, probably by Malcolm the Maiden in the middle of the twelfth century, of a Hospital on the bleak moor of Soltre or Soutra. As this was on a main road into

England the Hospital was a busy place, and gathered endowments to enable it carry on its good work. Two at least of these endowments are of interest to us. Some time in the thirteenth century Richard Germayne endowed the Hospital with the church of Lempitlaw, and a little later (1294) Thomas of Ercildoun, son and heir of Thomas the Rhymer, gave to it " totam meam terram in tenemento de Ercildoun." It would be nice to think that the patrimony of old Thomas the Rhymer was still supporting the cause of literature; unfortunately, whatever happened to it, Ercildoun is not in the hands of the Town Council.

When, in 1462, Mary of Gueldres founded the Collegiate Church and Hospital of the Holy Trinity, on ground now covered by the Waverley Station, she got the Hospital of Soltre and its possessions annexed to her new foundation. In 1585, Master Robert Pont, Provost of Trinity College and Hospital, under an agreement with the Magistrates, resigned the benefice " . . . with the parish kirk, parsonage and vicarage of Soltre and Lempitlaw . . ." to the Crown, by whom it was duly conveyed to the Town for the maintenance of Hospitals, College and Schools. I have not been able to discover on what principle, if any, the Town Council allocated these revenues as among the three classes of beneficiaries. The probability is that they used the money indiscriminately. Indeed it is not till 1640 that they make any attempt to separate the College and Schools account from the general accounts.

After the City had gone bankrupt the City Creditors Act of 1838 arranged that out of the sum to be paid annually to the City by the Leith Dock Commissioners, £2500 was to be applied by the Magistrates to the maintenance of the College and School. This figure was based on a Report by Mr Henry Labouchere, afterwards Lord Taunton, the Commissioner appointed by the Government to effect a settlement between the City and its creditors. He estimated that the College required about £2030 and the School about £400. This sum of £2500, of course, did not include the properties held by the Town for the College and School.

The final step was taken in 1861 when the College, or University, as it had then come to be styled, became master in its own financial household, and it was necessary to decide what the Town had to hand over and what it was to keep for the School. An Act of Parliament in that year assigned £2170 of the Dock money to the University and £330 to the School. The other properties were disposed of by two

Schedules annexed to the Act. Schedule B gave to the School:—

1. The Mortcloth Dues at Greyfriars			
2. Ground Annuals and Feu Duties in and about the City, amounting to	£9	3	0
3. Feu Duties in the County, amounting to	11	19	2
4. The Teinds in the Parishes of Sprouston, including Lempitlaw and Monimail, the tack duties of which presently amount together to	38	18	6
5. Property in N. College Street, the tack duties or rents of which presently amount to . . .	51	0	0
6. Bonds of Annuity by the City for £1800, being the price of the Patronages of Currie, Fala, and Wemyss, with the annuities payable thereon, amounting to .	54	0	0

It is item 4 which brings us back to our starting-point. The University, having got the major share of both funds and property, let us have the crumbs. The Sprouston teinds fortunately proved to be quite a substantial crumb. When they were definitely secured for the School some shrewd eye observed that the Duke of Buccleuch's lands in the parish had not been valued for teind for a long time. This was accordingly done, with the result that although the Duke took the matter to the

Court of Session he lost his case, and we now get some £250 from these same teinds.

The present state of the Endowment Fund, which for some time has been applied to the general expenditure of the School, irrespective of what the intentions of the original donors may have been, is as follows:—

1. Interest on Corporation Stock[1]	£206	6	10
2. Annuity from Corporation .	. 330	0	0
3. Mortcloth Dues (Greyfriars)[2]	. 2	2	0
4. Feu Duties and Teinds .	. 289	8	10
5. Temporary Loans Interest .	. 14	8	0
	£842	5	8

Our most recent bequest was made by Mr John Burns, W.S., who in 1942 left the sum of £1000 free of legacy duty to the Royal High School Club as trustees to make grants to School activities at their discretion.

[1] This represents those parts of items 2, 3, and 5 of Schedule B, which have been sold and the purchase price invested in Corporation Stock. It also includes item 6.

[2] In bygone days Edinburgh, like other towns, provided a mortcloth or pall to cover the coffin at a funeral and made a charge for it. This used to be a considerable source of revenue. In 1873 it brought in £32 19s., but burials in Greyfriars are now infrequent.

When we come to the endowed or permanent medals and prizes and other trophies we are on firmer ground. We take first the endowed medals and prizes in the order of their institution:—

1794, MURRAY now MACGREGOR Medal.— Endowed by a former pupil, Lieutenant-Colonel Peter Murray, adjutant of the Army in Bengal, whose grandfather, John Macgregor, had taken the surname of Murray owing to the proscription of the name Macgregor. This proscription was removed later, and in 1831 at the request of his nephew, Sir Evan Macgregor, the name of the medal was changed to Macgregor. The Medal is awarded to the Latin Dux of the School. Trustees, the Town Council.

1814, CITY Medal.—Instituted when, on the motion of Lord Provost Sir John Marjoribanks, it was unanimously resolved by the Council " that there be annually presented by the Town of Edinburgh to the boy at the head of the Greek Class a Medal of the same value as that annually presented to the Dux of the Latin Class."

1824, MACDONALD Medal.—Endowed by a former pupil, Colonel John Macdonald, son of Flora Macdonald, who gave £50 to endow a Medal for the Dux of the Third Class, the reason for his choice being that he was only one year at the School, and that in the Third Class. The nomenclature of the classes having changed, the Medal is now awarded to the Dux of the Junior School, who is one of the boys in Class 3A. Trustees, the Town Council.

1824, RITCHIE Medal.—Endowed by William Ritchie, who was a master from 1795 to 1818, when he retired. He bequeathed 100 guineas to provide an annual Gold Medal for the Dux of the class corresponding to that which he had taught. The Medal is now awarded to the Dux of Form II. Trustees, the Town Council.

1850, ROYAL HIGH SCHOOL CLUB Prize.— Originally given from subscriptions gathered at the Annual Meeting, this Prize is now endowed by the Club. Given in its earlier years for various subjects, it was in 1875 awarded to the Dux of the School, and since that date has been the premier award of the School.

1851, CARSON Medal.—Dr Aglionby-Ross Carson was a master in the School from 1806 to 1820, and Rector from 1820 to 1845, when he retired. In 1833 his old pupils subscribed for his portrait, which was presented to the School. The balance of the money subscribed was in 1851 vested in Trustees to endow an Annual Medal for English Composition, the income being paid to the Royal High School Club to administer. In 1928 the Trust was transferred to the Club. The Medal is awarded annually by competition open to the senior classes, the subject being chosen and the adjudicator appointed by the Club. The name of the winner is announced on Prize Day.

1857, BOYD Prize.—Dr James Boyd was a master in the School from 1829 to 1856. He died in office. His old pupils subscribed a sum of £100 to endow a book prize for the class taught by Dr Boyd's successor. The Prize is now awarded to the Dux of Form I. Trustees, the Town Council.

1865, MACMILLAN CLUB Prize. — John Macmillan was a master in the School from 1844 to 1867, when he retired. His pupils formed the Macmillan Club in 1863. In 1864 they gave a prize of books to Mr Macmillan's class. By the following year they had funded a sum of money to endow an Annual Prize. This for many years has taken the form of a gold watch, which is awarded to the Dux in English. In 1928 the surviving members of the Club appointed the Lord Provost, the Rector, and the Chairman of the Royal High School Club as Trustees of the Fund.

1868, DALTON Medal.—Endowed by Bailie George Cousin in memory of John Dalton, the famous chemist. In early years it is sometimes called the Dalton and sometimes the Cousin

Medal. It is awarded to the Dux of the School in Science. Trustees, the Town Council.

1868, TULLIS Medal.—Bailie Tullis was a former pupil of the School. From 1865 he gave annually a Gold Medal to the Dux of the senior Mathematical Class, and by his will he endowed the Medal. Trustees, the Rector and the senior Mathematics Master.

1872, INDIA Prize.—Endowed by a former pupil of the School, Dr George Smith, C.I.E., LL.D., Principal of Doveton College, Calcutta, later Editor of the *Friend of India*, and finally Foreign Mission Secretary of the Free Church of Scotland. It is open to the senior school and is awarded by special competition, the examiner being appointed by the Royal High School Club, as Trustees of the Fund.

1877, MACKAY Prizes.—Benjamin Mackay was a master from 1820 to 1843, when he retired. By his will he directed his trustees to invest the sum of £100 with the Town Council " to remain forever in their hands at 5 per cent. per annum, to enable them to award nine handsome book prizes for general knowledge, to found or endow a Gold Medal of the value of £5, and a bursary of £10 to be awarded quadrennially, and to bestow three handsome book prizes on the three best runners in a foot race of three heats from the High School gate

to the back or north wall of the playground."
In 1859 the Council declined to accept the
Trust as the income was obviously inadequate
for the purposes, but in 1861, presumably
having obtained a satisfactory legal opinion,
they accepted and invested the money, at that
date £115 5s. 9d. The marginal date gives
the first year in which there is record of these
Prizes being presented. The Prizes are at
present used for the Dux of Form IV., where
there is no endowed Medal, and for general
purposes, a discretion which seems amply war-
ranted by Benjamin Mackay's omnibus bequest.

1878, CARMICHAEL CLUB Medal. — John
Carmichael was a master from 1848 to 1870,
succeeding his uncle, William. He died in
office. His former pupils gave a prize annually
from 1868, and in the marginal year they
endowed a Medal which was originally given
for a knowledge of New Testament Greek.
The Medal is now given to the Dux of Form III.
Trustees, the Royal High School Club.

1910, JOHN MARSHALL Medal.—Dr Marshall
was Rector of the School from 1882 to 1909.
When he retired, the Royal High School Club
instituted this Medal for excellence in Latin,
Greek, and Mathematics. It is at present
awarded to the Dux in these subjects in Form
IV. The Medal is endowed by the Club.

1917, INCHES Prizes. — These Prizes were presented annually by a former pupil of the School, the late Sir Robert Kirk Inches, Lord Provost of the City. When Sir Robert was presented with his portrait by public subscription there was a surplus on the fund. Of this surplus £100 was allocated by the Committee of Subscribers, in accordance with the wishes of Sir Robert, to the endowment of these Prizes, which are awarded to the Duxes of the School in Chemistry and in Physics. Trustees, the Royal High School Club.

1924, ROYAL HIGH SCHOOL (LONDON) CLUB Prizes.—These Prizes have been given annually by the Club since 1924, one to the Dux of the School in Art and the other for an English Poem, the competition being open to the senior school.

1925, BRUCE Prize.—Endowed by a former pupil of the School, Edward Bruce, D.L., during his tenure of the office of Lord Dean of Guild. The Prize is awarded to the Dux of the School in History. Trustees, the Royal High School Club.

1925, CHISHOLM Prize. — Endowed by a former pupil of the School, Dr George Goudie Chisholm, who was Reader in Geography in the University of Edinburgh, and first winner of the Tullis Medal (1865). The Prize is awarded to the Dux of the School in Geography. Trustees, the Royal High School Club.

1928, NORMAN HOWARD SMALL MEMORIAL Prize.—Endowed by Mr W. A. Small in memory of his son, Norman Howard Small, who was killed in action, April 1915. The Prize is awarded to the Dux of the School in French. Trustees, the Royal High School Club.

1929, MUIR MEMORIAL Medal. — T. S. Muir was a former pupil of the School and a master from 1896 to 1898 and from 1900 to 1928. He died in office. His former pupils endowed this Medal, which is awarded to the Dux of Form V. Trustees, the Royal High School Club.

1932, SIR WALTER SCOTT CENTENARY Medal.—Instituted by the Royal High School Club to commemorate the centenary of the death of Sir Walter Scott, who was a pupil of the School from 1779 to 1783. The Medal bears a reproduction in miniature from the medallion of Sir Walter by Mr Pilkington Jackson. This Medal is endowed by the Club.

1932, SIR ALEXANDER STEVENSON Prize. When Sir Alexander Stevenson, formerly Lord Provost of the City, had his portrait presented by public subscription there was a surplus on the fund. At the request of Sir Alexander this surplus was used to endow a Prize, to be awarded to the boy who is *proxime accessit* to the Dux of the School. Trustees, the Town Council.

1934, ANDREW WILSON Prize.—Mr Andrew Wilson, a former Lord Dean of Guild and Master of the Merchant Company gave this Prize annually and endowed it by a legacy paid in 1943. It is awarded for Leadership. Trustees, the Royal High School Club.

1935, JOHN TURNER Prize.—Endowed by his former pupils on his retirement. He was senior Mathematical Master and Deputy Rector. Awarded to the Dux in Mathematics in Form V. Trustees, the Royal High School Club.

1938, CARSON Prize. Instituted by the Royal High School Club from the surplus of the Carson Medal Fund. Awarded to the Dux in English in Form V. Trustees, the Royal High School Club.

1939, JAMES A. GRANT Cup.—Presented by the Grant Club in memory of their Form Master who was Senior English Master. Awarded for Music.

1942, JOHN STOBIE Prize.—Endowed by Dr Athelstane Nobbs. Awarded for a Classical Paraphrase. Trustees, the Royal High School Club.

1945, NICOLL MEMORIAL Prize.—Endowed

by Mrs Nicoll in memory of her son, Alan, who was killed in the 1939-45 War. Awarded for Service. Trustees, the Royal High School Club.

There are several Prizes which are not endowed but which have been given annually, some over a long period of years.

1929, MUSIC PRIZES.—From 1929 to 1944 Mr James H. Thin presented seven prizes for Music to the Junior School and these are being continued by Mr J. Ainslie Thin.

1935, WILLIAM YOUNG MEMORIAL PRIZE.— Presented by his widow in memory of Mr. William Young, a former Senior Classical Master. Awarded to the Dux in Classics in Form V.

1935, JAMES M. MOORE MEMORIAL PRIZE.— Presented by his son Gilbert in memory of Mr James M. Moore, a former Senior Modern Languages Master, and later Professor of French in the University of Edinburgh. Awarded to the Dux in French in Form V.

1935, WILSON M. ROBERTSON PRIZE.—Presented by Mr Wilson M. Robertson originally for the Dux in Botany, and since 1941 as a Science Prize.

1937, R. S. WATSON PRIZE.—Presented by Mr. R. S. Watson. Awarded for Architectural Drawing.

1938, J. W. LOUDON Prize. Originally presented as one prize, it became two, Senior and Junior, in 1944, and has been continued by his widow. Awarded for Public Speaking.

1941, SANDERSON Prize.—Presented by the Rev. Mr. Sanderson in memory of J. S. and W. S. Sanderson. Awarded for a study of the poetry of Sir Walter Scott.

1942, WILLIAM KING GILLIES Prize.—Presented by Dr W. King Gillies, formerly Rector. Awarded for Ancient History.

1943, CHARLES H. BURROWS Prize.—Presented by Mr Charles H. Burrows, C.A. Awarded for Leadership in Athletics.

1947, JAMES GRAY MEMORIAL Prize.—Presented by his widow in memory of her husband who was Art Master and later Principal Lecturer in Art in the Moray House Training College. Awarded for Art Appreciation.

1948, SIR MALCOLM STEWART Prize.—Presented by Sir P. Malcolm Stewart, Bart. Awarded for Citizenship.

There are some Prizes which are given annually to this and other schools. These, with the dates when they were instituted, are The Edinburgh Sir Walter Scott Club Prizes (1897), The Robert Louis Stevenson Club Prize (1921), The Edinburgh and District Burns Clubs Association Prizes (1928), The

Bible Prizes presented by the Edinburgh Educational Endowments Scheme (1944), The S.S.P.C.A. Prize (1944), and the Margaret Burt Wright Prize (1945). With the exception of the Bible Prizes these are awarded for essays.

.   .   .   .   .

We come now to the Athletic Trophies. With the exception of the cricket bats and the golf medal these are all challenge trophies, in most cases accompanied by a medal to the winner.

1868, BATTING AND BOWLING AVERAGE Bats.—These were instituted by the Former Pupils' Cricket Club, and since then they have been given by various donors. From 1910 to 1939 they were presented by Mrs Clark, widow of the donor of the Colonel Clark Trophy. They were awarded for the best Batting and Bowling Averages in 1st XI. School Matches. Since 1939 they have lapsed.

1906, DOTT Shield.—Presented by Mr D. B. Dott and originally held by the Swimming Champion. In 1920 it was transferred to the 100 Yards Open Swimming Race and has since been held by the winner of that race.

1911, GAMES CHAMPIONSHIP Trophy.—Presented by the Former Pupils' Cricket Club. The Cup is held by the best athlete at the

SOME MEMORIALS

School Games and is awarded on a system of points for places in specified open events.

1911, GOLF Medal.—Presented annually by the Former Pupils' Golf Club, and awarded to the player who returns the best scratch score in the Medal Competition.

1912, COLONEL CLARK Trophy.—Colonel James Clark, Chairman of the Edinburgh School Board, and later, of the Edinburgh Education Authority, presented this Cup to be held by the best shot in the School.

1914, CRICHTON Trophy.—Presented by Mr J. D. Crichton, whose sons were at the School, as a Trophy for the Inter-Nation Squadron Swimming Race. In 1920 the Cup was transferred to the Nation Championship in Scholarship and Athletics combined, for which it has since been awarded.

1919, J. J. TROTTER MEMORIAL Bat.—J. J. Trotter was a former pupil of the School and a master from 1896 to 1917. He died in office. He was an international cricketer, and the author of a *History of the School*. Mr A. M. Trotter gave a sum of £50 to endow a Bat to be presented annually to the best all-round cricketer in the Under 15 XI., the team to which his brother had devoted special attention. Trustees, the Rector and the Convener of the School Cricket Committee.

1920, STRANG Trophy.—The Rev. R. C. Strang, a member of the School Board and of the Education Authority, took a keen interest in the School. When the Baths were reopened after the War he presented this Cup to be held by the Swimming Champion. It is awarded on a system similar to that which governs the Games Championship Trophy.

1927, McGEORGE (1919) Trophy. — A. McGeorge, when a pupil of the School, was, in 1919, first in all the events open to boys under 14 at the Inter-Scholastic Sports. In three of these events he broke the existing record. He presented this Cup to be held by the Games Champion under 14, the conditions being similar to those governing the other Championship Trophies.

1927, LIPTON ROSS Trophy.—Chief Constable and Mrs Ross presented this Cup in memory of their son, Thomas Lipton Ross, who died while a pupil of the School. It is held by the most efficient section in the Officers' Training Corps.

1928, INDIA Trophy.—Presented by the members of the Royal High School (India) Club, to be held by the Nation which gains the highest points for all-round efficiency in the Officers' Training Corps.

1928, MACKELVIE Trophy.—Presented by

a former pupil, Lieut.-Col. Maxwell MacKelvie, I.M.S., to be held by the best piper in the Officers' Training Corps.

1930, IV. R. (1921-2) Trophy.—Form IV. R. in the Session 1921-2 challenged all the other senior Forms to meet them in any kind of athletic contest and emerged victorious from the fray. Members of the Form presented this Cup for annual competition among the senior Forms. It is held by the Form which obtains the greatest number of points in team contests in the recognised branches of School athletic activity.

1931, MUIR MEMORIAL Trophy.—When the Muir Memorial Medal was endowed, the Committee of Subscribers was left with a balance in hand. As Mr Muir was one of the founders of the Nation system, and had for a long time managed the Annual Games, this balance was used to purchase a Cup to be held by the Nation gaining the highest aggregate of points at the Games, under a scheme prepared by the Games Committee.

1932, LAWSON Trophy.—Presented by Mr George Lawson, an original member of the Former Pupils' Golf Club, and held by the Champion Nation at Golf.

1933, JAMES AIKMAN SMITH Trophy.— Presented by the Royal High School Club, in memory of Mr James Aikman Smith, who was for forty years Treasurer of the Club, and for many years Secretary, and, later, President of the Scottish Rugby Union. It is held by the Games Champion under 16. A miniature of the Cup is presented to the winner.

1938, SANDERSON Cup.—Presented by Mrs Crawford, daughter of Mr Mark Sanderson. Awarded to the Champion Nation in the Junior School.

1943, JAMES GORDON BROWN Cups.—Presented by his mother, Mrs Learmonth, in memory of her son, a former Swimming Champion of the School, who was killed in the 1939-1945 war. They are awarded for swimming, one to the Senior School and one to the Junior School.

1946, GILMOUR Trophy.—Presented by his father and aunt in memory of James L. Gilmour, a former Captain of the School and of the XV, who was killed in the 1939-1945 War. Awarded to the Champion Nation in Rugby.

·   ·   ·   ·   ·

From time to time there have been prizes of a temporary nature. Our printed Reports go back to 1845, and from them we learn that frequently, though not invariably, the Lord Provost, the College Bailie, whose modern counterpart is the Chairman of the Education

Committee, and other Councillors presented special prizes. It is evident that members of the Town Council took a practical interest in the doings of the School. In many cases, of course, the donors had themselves been educated here: Bailie Tawse, who gave a Medal for several years, was a Vice-President of the Royal High School Club. Other former pupils unconnected with the Council also appear from time to time. Lord Neaves, who in 1814 was Macgregor Medallist, in 1874 presented the best classical scholar with a complete set of Blackwood's *Ancient Classics for English Readers*—a thoughtful gift. Limits of space preclude the giving of a complete list, but some items may be mentioned.

A notable benefaction is recorded in a letter from the City Members of Parliament to the Lord Provost under date 25th July 1837. Hitherto the prizes had been presented by the Town Council out of the revenues assigned to the School. But the Town had gone bankrupt and the Trustees would not allow the money to be spent in this way. Here is the letter of the Members of Parliament:—

" MY LORD,
         Understanding that in consequence of the embarrassed state of the affairs of the City the money which used to be devoted to giving prizes to

the youth of the High School can no longer be supplied, we hope we may be allowed to express our warm feeling for the success of the High School by giving such sums as may be necessary for providing the Annual Prizes, and we have thought it proper to make this communication to you and to the Town Council as Patrons of the High School. We have, etc.,

J. ABERCROMBY.
J. CAMPBELL."

The Council gratefully accepted this generous offer.

The Philp Medal (1824) is an interesting award. William Bain gained the Murray (now Macgregor) Medal in 1809. After a brilliant University career he died in 1815. His uncle, Mr Patrick Philp, who was greatly attached to his nephew, died in 1822. By his will he left instructions for a Gold Medal to be presented to the Rector's Class, to be worn daily by the Dux. The Medal bore this inscription, " Numisma Philpianum, condiscipulorum duci in classe ipsa quotidie gestandum." It is to be regretted that this unique trophy has disappeared.

From 1850 to 1860 the Earl of Camperdown, First President of the Royal High School Club, gave the Camperdown Prize annually. In 1857 the French Consul presented a prize. A " Citizens' Medal " figures in 1858.

Several medals or prizes were presented for varying periods by Class Clubs. In some cases these were ultimately endowed.

.   .   .   .   .

We have now to deal with gifts other than prizes or trophies. The Library has been a frequent recipient of such gifts. In 1801 George Grindlay, merchant in Edinburgh, presented his collection of books and maps to the School. More recently Mr J. S. Ramsay presented his historical library, and the latest addition is a complete set of the volumes of the Scottish History Society, presented by Dr James Watt.

The marble bust of King Edward as Prince of Wales was presented by a Committee of Subscribers, mainly, but not wholly, former pupils, the indefatigable Bailie Colston acting as Secretary. It is the work of Mr (afterwards Sir John) Steell, Her Majesty's Sculptor for Scotland, the pedestal being designed by David Bryce, R.S.A. It was unveiled on the day observed as the Prince's twenty-first birthday, 10th November 1862. Out of a subscription of £271 17s. 1d. the pupils contributed £64 14s. 1d. The Town Council are Trustees of the bust " for behoof of the High School."

Our valuable collection of portraits and engravings of former masters and pupils has been acquired at various times. The original portrait of Adam, by Raeburn, having been replaced in 1864, largely at the instigation of Leonard Horner, by a copy painted by a former pupil, F. Cruickshank, it occurred to some former pupils and other friends to form in 1865 a Royal High School Commemorative Association, for the purpose of procuring pictures, engravings and busts for the School. Bailie Colston, of course, was Secretary. In this way we acquired a copy of the Raeburn Scott (also by F. Cruickshank), the Erskine and many others. In more recent times the Royal High School Club has taken up the work of the now defunct Commemorative Association; individual donors have contributed to the collection; and the School Fund, derived from the proceeds of concerts and other functions, has also assisted, its latest contribution being the marble replica of the Chantrey bust of Sir Walter which now adorns the Hall.

On the centenary, in 1929, of the opening of the present School building, a bronze medallion of Thomas Hamilton, R.S.A., the architect of the School, was placed in the east court of the School, and a replica on the gravestone of Hamilton in the Old Calton burying-ground. The medallion was the work of the late

D. C. Francis, A.R.S.A. This was a gift from the pupils of 1929. A similar gift was made by the pupils of 1932 when, on the occasion of the Scott Centenary, a medallion of Sir Walter, the work of Mr Pilkington Jackson, was placed in the west court.

Two gifts are in daily use. The chair used by the Rector in the Hall is the chair used by King Edward when, as Prince of Wales, he presented the prizes in 1859. What happened to it in the interval I am unable to state; eventually it came into the possession of Mr Neilson, who presented it to the School in 1924. And the brass lectern which has replaced the old red-baize covered reading-desk that stood in front of the Rector's chair is the gift of two well-known High School men, Dr Robert Thin and Mr James Hay Thin.

The outstanding gift is the War Memorial. This took the form of a Roll of Honour, a Memorial Porch, and a Memorial Field, and was naturally the joint contribution of many former and present pupils and masters. The Memorial Porch, inside the south wall of the Hall, was designed by the late Mr James Gray, A.R.I.B.A. It is of Skye and Iona marbles, the unhewn marble blocks being the gift of Dr James Watt. It is flanked by brass panels bearing the names of the 183 former pupils who gave their lives. The bronze handle on the Memorial Door was a gift from the late Professor Robert Donaldson.

The Memorial Field was acquired by a Feu Contract between the Duke of Abercorn and Dr James Watt, recorded on 25th September 1919, while the entrance from the Portobello Road and the adjacent houses were acquired by Dr Watt separately, and a Discharge obtained later from the Duke, freeing the entrance and buildings from feu-duty. The whole of these were later transferred (at a reduced price) by him to the following Trustees: The Lord Provost, the Convener of the Education Committee, the Rector, the President of the Royal High School Club, the Vice-President of the Royal High School Athletic Club (all *ex-officiis*), a nominee of the Royal High School Club, a nominee of the Royal High School Athletic Club, and Dr Watt. In order that funds might be available for the equipment of the field, arrangements were made for a substantial portion of the purchase price being paid in instalments. The last of these was paid at Whitsunday 1930, and the work of the Memorial Committee brought to a close.

A notable acquisition to the field is the Pavilion presented by the Education Authority and opened on 25th July 1925 by H.R.H. the Prince Henry. Replicas of the Memorial Panels, the gift of Dr Watt, have been placed in the hall of the Pavilion. Later in the year an additional strip of ground at the south end, about three-quarters of an acre in area, was acquired from the Town Council at a cost of £127 1s. A special fund, amounting to £322 2s. 2d., was raised by subscription to meet this cost and to fence the field. Since then trees have been planted by former Captains of Cricket or Football or Games Champions, a commemorative tree in the first instance being planted for every former Captain or Games Champion who was killed in the War. To meet capital expenditure on the ground a Sale of Work, which realised £1589 17s. 1d., was held in 1927. This money was vested in Trustees, and has been gradually expended on ground improvement, not including the Stand, the money for which was raised by an issue of debentures.

In successive years from 1935 Dr James Watt presented to the Library the publications of the Scottish History Society and the Scottish Text Society including all the volumes previous to that year.

1936. Mr William Watson presented four oak panels which were placed on each side of the middle doors in Hall. Those on the west side bear the names and dates of the Captains of the School while those on the east side bear the names and dates of the Rectors.

1938. A number of Former Pupils including the Clubs in London, India and Malaya, subscribed £128 9s. to equip the O.T.C. Band with uniform and an additional set of bagpipes.

1938. Mr Alexander Naismith Mouat, C.A., Comptroller-General of the Province of British Columbia, 1917-29, presented an unique collection of Canadian Trophies. These are now housed in the Geography Department.

1939. The Royal High School Club in India presented to the O.T.C. a leopard skin and a silver baton and staff.

1939. Messrs Donald Grant and Sons, all Former Pupils, presented the oak cabinets in which our Trophies are displayed in Hall.

1945. The J.T.C. received the gift of a set of bapgipes bearing this inscription: " Presented to the Royal High School by his mother and sister in memory of Captain Ian A. Nicoll, 1/2nd Gurkha Rifles. Killed in action at Cassino, February 1944."

1947. Present and Former Pupils subscribed £2,000 to present the School with an Organ in Hall. Reference is made to this on p. 39.

One contingent gift falls to be recorded. In 1940 the Royal High School Club organised a subscription and presented Dr King Gillies and Mr Ross with their portraits, the former by David Allison, R.S.A., and the latter by E. S. Lumsden, R.S.A. Both recipients intimated their intention of ultimately presenting these portraits to the Royal High School Club to be hung in the School, and Mr Ross has now implemented this undertaking.

Another War has given cause for another Memorial, and again Former Pupils, Parents, Staff and Present Pupils have provided the funds. This time the Memorial takes the form of a Roll of Honour, Stained Glass Windows at the North end of the Hall and a Memorial Gateway and avenue at Jock's Lodge. The three windows are the work of Mr William Wilson, R.S.A. The oak work under the windows and the panels bearing the names of the fallen are designed by a Former Pupil, Mr William G. Dey, A.R.I.B.A. The oak work is being carried out by Messrs Donald Grant and Sons and the panels by Messrs. Whytock and Reid. The windows will be dedicated on 5th July 1949. Work at Jock's Lodge is in progress. The gateway has been designed by Mr Dey. The construction work on the avenue is being carried out by another Former Pupil, Mr R. S. Watson, and the wrought-iron gates by Mr Hadden.

It now remains to record the Bursaries and Scholarships in connection with the School. These are not numerous.

1871, SIBBALD Bursaries.—John Robertson Sibbald, M.D., F.R.S.E., was a doctor in practice in Edinburgh, who died in 1868. By his will he directed his trustees " to found or endow ten bursaries for sons of medical men or other respectable citizens to enable them to attend the High School or University." Unfortunately he left " a mass of writings of a testamentary nature," and the matter had to be cleared up by the Court of Session. As a result five bursaries of £20 each per annum were allotted to the School. Trustees, the President of the Royal College of Surgeons, the Principal of the University and the Rector of the Royal High School (*ex officiis*), with three individual trustees.

1880, DONALDSON Bursary.—Dr James Donaldson was a master from 1856 to 1866, Rector from 1866 to 1882, and subsequently Principal of St Andrews University. The Donaldson Club founded this Bursary. When in 1884 the Club came to an end it transferred the funds, at that date £300 17s. 10d., to a body of five Trustees, who, in 1913, handed over the funds, by that time amounting to £465 0s. 7d., to the Edinburgh School Board.

The original subjects of competition were Latin, Greek and English, but these have been extended, and the Bursary is at present open to boys entering the Fourth Form. Trustees, the Town Council.

1881, ROBERTSON Bursary.—John Robertson was a schoolmaster at Preston. By his will (1830) he left all his money to establish and maintain a school in or near Edinburgh for the education of boys for mercantile pursuits. In 1880 his Trustees obtained a Provisional Order permitting them to sell the school buildings, invest the proceeds in heritable securities and make over the sum so invested, together with all the other funds of the estate, amounting to about £1316 similarly invested, to be held by the School Board of Edinburgh for the purpose of providing by competitive examination a bursary or bursaries for pupils from the public or other elementary schools entering the Royal High School. Trustees, the Town Council.

1929, SIR DAVID YULE MEMORIAL Scholarships.—Sir David Yule was a pupil of the School from 1868 to 1874. He went to India, where he built up what was probably the largest business in that country. He died in 1928. His widow, Dame Annie Yule, in 1930 gave a sum of £4000 to endow a Scholarship or Scholarships of the annual value of at least £40, tenable for a period of four years. The Scholarships are tenable at a British or other University approved by the Governors, and the period may, in their discretion, be extended. The Governors are the Lord Provost, the Rector, and a nominee of the Royal High School Club. Trustees, the Town Council.

Bursaries which used to exist but have now lapsed are the Marshall-Kirkliston Bursary, and the Heriot High School Bursaries. Mr Robert Marshall, merchant in Edinburgh, by a Trust Disposition and Settlement dated 10th February 1865, bequeathed the residue of his estate to Trustees to be held for the purpose of relieving indigent persons and for the promotion of education through Schools and Colleges. In 1878 the Trustees instituted a Bursary Scheme. This was reorganised in 1906-7, and three Bursaries of £12 each per annum were allotted to boys in the parish of Kirkliston, not over twelve years of age, to enable them to attend the Royal High School. Owing to the growth of facilities for secondary education in West Lothian the scheme was again altered, and after 1924 no bursaries were awarded to pupils going to the Royal High School.

Following on the Educational Endowments (Scotland) Act of 1882, by which George

Heriot's Hospital became George Heriot's School and the Heriot Free Schools were given up, a scheme was framed whereby not less than five Heriot Bursaries of an annual value not exceeding £20, tenable at the Royal High School for three years, with a permissible extension for another two years, were established. These were to be awarded to pupils attending State-aided Schools in Edinburgh. At the same time £300 was to be devoted to Heriot High School Bursaries of £20 (later £30), tenable for two years, to be awarded to pupils of the Royal High School, and nine Heriot High School University Bursaries of the yearly value of £30, tenable for three years, with a permissible extension to four years, were also established. Modifications were made later, and finally in 1922 the scheme was recast, and these High School Bursaries disappeared. They were first awarded in 1886.

There was another reorganisation in 1936 when, as a result of the Educational Endowments (Scotland) Commission's Report and the Act of 1935 which followed it, a Royal High School Endowments Sub-Committee consisting of five members of the Education Committee and two representatives of the Royal High School Club was set up. Under the scheme Royal High School Exhibitions to the University were instituted. Since then three new Bursaries have been founded.

1937. MORRISON Bursary.—Endowed by Mr John Paton Morrison.

1938. CARSON Bursary.—Instituted by the Royal High School Club from the surplus of the Carson Medal Fund. Tenable for two years. Awarded in Form IV. Trustees, the Royal High School Club.

1948. SIR MALCOLM STEWART, BART., Exhibition.—Tenable for two years at an University. Presented by Sir P. Malcolm Stewart, Bart.

REGULATIONS FOR THE EXTERNAL DISCIPLINE OF THE HIGH SCHOOL OF EDINBURGH

(These Regulations were drafted by Drs Boyd and Gunn, and approved by the Rector and Masters in 1846. Since then, in whole or part, they have been read in Hall at the commencement of each Session.)

The Rector and Masters of the High School feel it to be their duty to remind the ingenuous Youth educated in this venerable Institution, that the moral well-being of man is paramount even to his intellectual advancement. You are, accordingly, affectionately admonished to seek that fear of the Lord, which is the beginning of wisdom; and while you are not slothful in business, in the days of your youth to remember your Creator, in the two great departments of duty—love of God, and love to man.

It is incumbent on those entrusted with your education to see that you are trained to conduct yourselves in all the various relationships of life as Christians and as gentlemen. In addition to the direct bearing which the religious instruction you here receive has upon this great object, the branches of polite learning in which you are disciplined, will, no doubt, contribute to this result. You will, besides, reflect that with you rests the reputation of the School, not for scholarship merely, but for habits of Christian virtue and manly urbanity. Such considerations, it is hoped, will not fail to produce among you a high-toned morality combined with a polite demeanour. But you are also warned, that duty, if not voluntarily discharged, must, for the common safety, be enforced by penalties.

The internal discipline of each class is confided to its own individual Teacher. With regard to the external discipline, it is impossible to lay down such regulations as shall embrace every case. But the following Rules comprehend the duties mainly to be enforced; and other violations of the great principles of right, while you are earnestly warned against them, will be dealt with as each case may require:—

I. All flagrant violations of the moral law, lying, dishonesty, swearing, obscenity, immodesty of every kind, are forbidden under the severest penalties, as most displeasing to God, degrading to your own nature, and hateful in the eyes of men.

II. It is proper, though, it is hoped, hardly

necessary, to enjoin upon you cleanliness of person and dress, as seemly in itself, and productive of health and comfort.

III. Punctuality and regularity of attendance are essential to your improvement, and will be rigidly exacted, except for necessary causes.

IV. You are forbidden, while going to or from School, to do anything which is annoying to your fellow-citizens, which is unworthy of the education you are receiving, or which may bring the discipline of the School into disrepute.

V. The Masters and Teachers are entitled to respectful behaviour, not only from their own, but from all the pupils of the School.

VI. You are enjoined to behave courteously to your schoolfellows, loving your neighbours as yourselves, in honour preferring one another. The seniors are enjoined to comport themselves in a kindly manner to those who are younger and weaker, and any attempt at oppression will be regarded as a proof of unmanly spirit, and energetically repressed.

VII. There is no desire to interfere unduly with your amusements; on the contrary, you will receive every encouragement and protection, compatible with a proper discipline, in all manly and in all healthful sports. But you are forbidden to engage in such amusements as are injurious to the property or person of others, or are hurtful or dangerous to yourselves.

VIII. Fighting, and such amusements as naturally lead to irritation and violence, are forbidden.

IX. Disturbing any of the Classes in the course of your games, or by shouting, staring in at the windows, or in any other way, is peremptorily forbidden.

X. The splendid building provided by the munificence of the City for the education of its youth, it will be your pride to preserve from injury. All climbing on any part of the building, all playing against it with marbles, balls or anything else, is, on that ground forbidden. You are, also, cautioned against carrying on any of your amusements so near to the building, as to expose you to the hazard of breaking any of the windows.

XI. You are required to abstain from the offensive and vulgarising practice of writing on the walls; and from defacing in any way any part of the building.

XII. No bludgeons, sticks or other instruments that may be employed in games or otherwise, so as to injure the building by chipping off the edges of the mason-work or otherwise, are to be brought within the grounds.

XIII. You are earnestly desired to assist in preserving for the common benefit, what has been expressly provided for that purpose. This you can do by your advice and example. And you are forbidden, under pain of severe penalties, wantonly or carelessly to waste the water, to injure the watercocks, or anything else provided for the public convenience.

XIV. You are reminded that, in addition to the punishment due for any injury committed against property, your liability for damages occasioned by the transgression of the Rules, will, on all occasions, be strictly enforced.

XV. You are absolutely forbidden to climb on, or run along any of the walls, or climb on or over any of the railings, or to leave or to come to School by any other than the ordinary modes of egress and ingress; and it is necessary from the vicinity of pleasure-grounds to one part of the wall, to warn you against making your way into them, on any pretext whatever. You must submit to occasional losses at your amusements, rather than infringe the rights of property.

XVI. Missiles of every description, whether stones, gravel, or snow-balls, are absolutely forbidden.

XVII. No gunpowder, fireworks, or fire-arms of any description, are permitted to be brought within the grounds, under penalty of confiscation, and such punishment as may be necessary.

XVIII. In addition to the spacious playground provided by the Patrons for your recreation, you have the free range of the Calton Hill, at fit opportunities. You are only forbidden, for the purpose of securing your own safety, to go on that precipitous part of the Hill, immediately behind the School, situated between the two lower walks.

XIX. In your enjoyment of this, and of all your privileges, you are warned against molesting or injuring others in any way. You are especially forbidden to come into hostile contact by throwing stones, or otherwise, with any other boys, or assemblages of boys, and this, notwithstanding any pretext whatever.

XX. With such an ample field for recreation, you can have no excuse for playing on the streets while on your road to or from School, or at your play hours. This can only be done at your own risk, and to the molestation of others. You must not form slides on the streets or roads leading to the School, as manifestly injurious to the public safety.

XXI. Nothing can be more improper or hurtful to the character of the School, than that, congregated on the edge of a great thoroughfare, you should abuse your position, to annoy or injure the public, by shouting or throwing missiles, or by any other means. This will be prevented by severe penalties. And, more especially, you are warned against yielding to the childish excitement produced by the appearance of the military, as complaints have been made of violations of this necessary rule.

XXII. The Rector, the Masters, and Teachers, along with the Janitor, are authorised to mark and report in the proper quarters for enforcement, all violations of these Rules, to whatever class the violators may belong.

In conclusion, you are entreated to bear carefully in mind the spirit in which these Regulations are framed, and the great objects which they are intended to serve. Our highest delight is to train your youthful minds, and to accustom you to such habits of intellectual and moral discipline, that you shall go forth from our Halls, fitted and prepared by your acquirements and your virtues, to maintain and extend the fame of your *Alma Mater*, to prove valuable members of the commonwealth, and to adorn the doctrine of God our Saviour in all things.

ATHLETIC RECORDS

Definite records of the early days in the various branches of athletics are hard to come by. But for the good offices of two former pupils, Mr Chalmers Anderson and the Secretary of the Former Pupils' Cricket Club, Mr A. A. C. Dickson, the following statistics would have been even less complete than they are. Additional information will be gratefully received and preserved.

CRICKET

Former Pupils

REPRESENTATIVE PLAYERS.

Adair, T. J. . . *v.* An Irish XI., 1898.

Buchanan, A. . . *v.* United South of England XI., 1872.

Cunningham, W. C. *v.* United South of England XI., 1872-3.

Johnston, T. . . *v.* United All - England XI., 1887; M.C.C., 1898; Lancashire, 1899; Gloucestershire, 1902; Surrey*

Lawson, T. M. . *v.* Ireland and Wales, 1923; S. Africa, 1924.

Macgrecgor, A. V. . *v.* Surrey.*

* Dates for these matches are not available.

McTavish, A. K.	. *v.* Ireland 1929-30-31-36-37-38-39.
	v. South Africa, 1929.
	v. Australia, 1930.
	v. New Zealand 1931, 1937 (2).
	v. All India, 1932.
	v. South America, 1932.
	v. M.C.C., 1934-39.
	v. Sir J. Cahn's XI, 1936-37 (2); 1938-39 (2).
	v. Yorkshire, 1937-38 (a total of 24 caps).
Muirhead, I. .	. *v.* *
Murrie, R. B. .	. *v.* All-England XI., 1876.
Sanderson, F. .	. *v.* United South of England XI., 1877; Daft's England XI., 1880; Philadelphians, 1884.
Sanderson, G. .	. *v.* Daft's England XI., 1880.
Sanderson, J. .	. *v.* United South of England XI., 1872.
Smith, D. L. A.	. *v.* Australia.*
Smith, W. W. .	. *v.* United South of England XI. 1872.
Thomson, C. .	. *v.* All-England XI., 1876.
Trotter, J. J. .	. *v.* *
Watt, N. . .	. *v.* All-England XI., 1876; United South of England XI., 1877.
Wilson, E. W. .	. *v.* Ireland 1936.
Wood, A. L. .	. *v.* Australia, 1880, 1882; M.C.C., 1880.

President of the Scottish Cricket Union, D. Connel, 1923.

Cricket, unlike Football, lends itself to individual records and some of those which have been preserved are given here.

* Dates for these matches are not available.

BATTING.

Highest Score by XI., 329 for 8, *v.* Grange, 1912

Averages: T. Johnston, 10 inn.; av. 66.6; 1891.

T. Johnston, 4 inn.; av. 125; 1893.

A. K. McTavish, 12 inn.; av. 77.8; 1930.

(The highest average for 1930 in Scottish Cricket.)

Aggregates: T. M. Lawson, 695 runs; 1913.

E. W. Wilson, 783 runs; 1934.

For first wicket: E. W. Wilson and W. D. Emslie, 197, *v.* Institution F.P., 1933.

For second wicket: T. Johnston and W. R. Gibson, 252, *v.* Brunswick, 1894.

For tenth wicket: F. G. Bucher and W. C. A. Ross, 108, *v.* Dalkeith, 1909.

First century at Holyrood: F. R. Sanderson, *v.* Edinburgh University, 1881.

First century at Jock's Lodge: A. K. McTavish, *v.* P.P. XI., 1926.

BOWLING.

1877. Angus Buchanan: 10 wkts., all clean bowled, *v.* Edinburgh Academicals.

1886. J. L. Buist: 9 wkts. for 0 runs, *v.* 2nd Academicals.

1889. J. J. Trotter: 5 wkts. in 5 consecutive balls, *v.* Galashiels.

1890. A. V. Macgregor: 5 wkts. for 6 runs, *v.* Carlton, 6 wkts. for 10 runs, *v.* Brunswick.

J. J. Trotter: 8 wkts. for 11 runs, *v.* Clydesdale. (Trotter's bowling average, 104 wkts., av. 5.12 is the F.P. record.)

1891. J. J. Trotter: 6 wkts. for 12 runs, *v.* Dalkeith.

1895. J. J. Trotter: 10 wkts. for 20 runs (opening match); 6 wkts. for 10 runs, *v.* Cupar; 6 wkts. for 5 runs, *v.* Dalkeith.

(In each of these consecutive matches, Trotter had a " hat trick." The following Saturday,

BOWLING—*continued*.

the professional, Hainsworth, took 4 wickets
with successive balls.)

1907. W. C. A. Ross: 7 wkts. for 8 runs, *v.* Burnt-
island.

1936. P. F. Hutton took his 500th wicket for the F.P.
1st XI.

1946. F. O. Thomas: 9 wkts. (8 clean bowled) for
25 *v.* Edinburgh University.

Nat Watt was Captain of the Club for seven years
running. In three consecutive years his team won 72
matches, lost 8, and drew 10.

In post-war cricket, E. W. Wilson has scored the
largest number of centuries (14), for the F.P. XI.

Present Pupils

BATTING.

Average: E. W. Wilson, 14 inn.; av. 41.6; 1924.

Aggregate: G. A. Smith, 632 runs; 1932.

For first wicket: E. W. Wilson and W. A. Stoker, 153,
v. Institution; 1924.

For third wicket: F. O. Thomas and A. R. Haddow,
115, *v.* Perth Academy; 1934.

First century at Jock's Lodge: E. W. Wilson, Rest of
School *v.* Picts, 1923.

E. W. Wilson won the batting average in three successive years, 1923-4-5.

In the East *v.* West Day Schools Match (1925) E. W.
Wilson and R. Seath made 88 for the tenth wicket.
Wilson carried his bat for 101 out of a total of 157
for 9 wickets.

BOWLING.

1906. J. C. Dickson: 97 wkts.; av. 6.3.

1934. K. A. R. Gomez: 7 wkts. for 2 runs *v.* Borough-
muir.

RUGBY FOOTBALL

INTERNATIONAL PLAYERS.

Brewis, N. T.[1]	.	E. 1876-8-9-80; I. 1879-80.
Buchanan, A.	.	E. 1871.
Bucher, A. M.[2]	.	E. 1897.
Davidson, R. S.	.	E. 1893.
Duke, A.	.	I. and W. 1888-9-90.
Emslie, W. D.	.	F. 1930; I. 1932.
Ferguson, W. G.	.	N.S.W. 1927; E., I. and W. 1928; F. 1928.
Gibson, W. R.	.	E. and I. 1891-2-3-4-5; W. 1892-3-4-5.
Gunn, A. W.	.	I.,W. and S.A. 1912; F. 1912-13.
Hume, J.	.	E., I. and W. 1921; F. 1912-20-21-22.
Laing, A. D.	.	E. 1914-20; I. and W. 1914-20; F. 1920-21.
McGlashen, T. P.		E. 1947; I. 1947.
MacIntyre, I.[3]	.	E., I. and W. 1890-1.
McLaren, E.	.	E., I. and W. 1923; F. 1923-4.
McLean, D. I.	.	E. 1947; I. 1947.
Macdonald, W. A.		E. and I. 1892; W. 1889.
Masters, W. H.[4]		E. 1880; I. 1879-80.
Menzies, H. F.	.	E. and W. 1894; I. and W. 1893.
Morrison, M. C.	.	E. 1896-7-8-9-1900-1-2-4; I. 1896-7-8-9-1901-2-3-4; W. 1896-9-1900-1-2-3-4.
Penman, W. M.	.	I. 1939.
Petrie, A. G.	.	E. 1873-4-5-6-7-8-9-80; I. 1877-9-80.
Park, J.	.	W. 1934.
Ross, A.	.	E. 1905; I. and W. 1905-09.
Sanderson, G. A.	.	E. and W. 1907; I. 1907-8.
Simpson, J. W.[5]	.	E. 1893-4-5-7-9; I. 1893-4-5-6; W. 1894-5-6-9.

[1] Also Edinburgh Institution. [3] Also Edinburgh Academy.
    ,, Fettes College. [4] ,, Edinburgh Institution.
    ,, Dollar Institution.

INTERNATIONAL PLAYERS—*continued*.

Tait, P. W. . . E. 1935.

Veitch, J. P. . . E. 1882-4-6; I. 1883-4-5; W. 1884.

Wilson, G. R. . E. 1886-90; I. 1890-1; W. 1890

Wood, A. T. . E. 1873-4-5.

PRESIDENTS OF THE SCOTTISH RUGBY UNION.

1879-80— A. Buchanan.   1904-5—J. W. Simpson.

1881-82— A. G. Petrie.   1926-7—J. Aikman Smith.

1885-86— N. T. Brewis.   1931-2—J. C. Sturrock.

1899-1900—I. MacIntyre.   1934-5—M. C. Morrison.

1902-3— R. S. Davidson.

T. P. McGlashen played in the " Services " International v. England, 1945. He and D. I. McLean played in the combined Edinburgh and Glasgow XV. v. Australia, 1946.

In 1883-4 the F.P. XV. won the Championship with a record of 11 won, 3 drawn, and 1 lost.

In 1933-4 the F.P. XV. shared the Championship with Hillhead High School. Their record was 25 games, won 21, lost 4; points for, 398; against, 194.

J. Aikman Smith was Secretary of the Scottish Rugby Union from 1890-1914, and acting Secretary 1914-19.

J. G. Y. Buchanan was Secretary of the Edinburgh District Rugby Union for 24 years.

Nat Watt, as at cricket, was captain of the Club for seven years running. In the three seasons from 1881-4, " Nat's lambs " lost only 5 matches.

Angus Buchanan scored the first try in the first International match (Scotland *v.* England, 1871).

ROYAL HIGH SCHOOL

ATHLETICS

Former Pupils

Duncan, D. S.: One Mile Champion of Scotland, 1883-4-5-6-91. He was the first holder of the mile championship. In 1888 he created a Scottish Native Record for the mile, 4 mins. 28 secs., which stood for several years. He also held the records for 2 and 3 miles.

McMichael, D. C.: He was the first champion of the Edinburgh Harriers. One Mile Champion of Scotland, 1890. He held the record for 1000 yards for several years.

Paisley, C. J. F.: Quarter-Mile Champion of Scotland, 1887. In this year he twice equalled the record for the quarter mile.

Seton, M. C. C.: Half-Mile Champion of Scotland, 1895.

Smith, G. A.: Athletic Blue, Edinburgh University, 1933-4; Cross-Country Blue, Edinburgh University, 1932-3, 1933-4; Inter-University Mile and Half-Mile Champion, 1933; Edinburgh University Half-Mile Champion, 1933; Edinburgh University and F.P. Union Half-Mile Champion, 1933; Inter-University Half-Mile Champion, 1934.

Watson, W. A.: Athletic Blue, Edinburgh University, 1919-20-21. Inter-University Mile Champion, 1920; Edinburgh University Mile Champion, 1919; Edinburgh University Three Mile Champion, 1919-20.

Present Pupils

OPEN RECORDS AT SCHOOL GAMES.

Throwing the Cricket Ball: H. Strachan (1903), 109 yards.

Putting the Weight: T. P. L. McGlashan (1943), 36 ft. 1 1/2 ins.

High Leap: G. M. Bucher (1887), W. R. Britee (1948), 5 ft. 4 ins.

Long Leap: W. R. Britee (1948), 20 ft. 4 1/2 ins.

ATHLETIC RECORDS

120 Yards Hurdles: G. R. Gunn (1929), 16 3/5 secs.

100 Yards: G. P. T. Barclay (1946), W. R. Britee (1948), 10.5 secs.

220 Yards: H. T. S. Rankin (1947), 23.7 secs.

Quarter-Mile: R. W. Gollogley (1935), 54.2 secs.

Half-Mile: G. A. Smith (1932), 2 mins. 6 4/5 secs.

One Mile: A. C. Nicoll (1935), 4 mins. 48 2/5 secs.

Discus: H. N. Henriksen (1949), 116 ft. 10 1/2 ins.

Javelin: J. Cruickshank (1948), 135 ft. 6 ins.

Pole Vault: W. R. Britee (1948), 9 ft. 4 ins.

J. Brewis was the founder and first President of the S.A.A.A. (1883). D. S. Duncan was Honorary Secretary from 1885-1925.

INTER-SCHOLASTIC GAMES CHAMPIONS

Open.

100 Yards: T. Catto, 1911.

440 Yards: T. Catto, 1911; T. Mather, 1928.

One Mile: C. F. Henry, 1913; W. A. Watson, 1918 (record); J. Halliday, 1919; C. D. Golding, 1922; G. A. Smith, 1931 and 1932.

High Jump: A. E. McIntosh (eq.), 1912 and 1913; G. E. M. Govan, 1915 and 1916.

Broad Jump: G. E. M. Govan, 1916.

Throwing the Cricket Ball: H. Dodson, 1913.

Relay Races: 1918, 1919, 1933, 1934.

Under 16.

880 Yards: W. Watson, 1916.

120 Yards Hurdles: J. G. Black, 1912; G. E. M. Govan, 1914; A. Dobbie, 1920.

High Jump: M. Edelman (eq.), 1912.

Broad Jump: R. N. Fairgrieve, 1901; G. E. M. Govan, 1914; E. McGregor, 1915.

Under 14.

100 Yards: J. Elder, 1914; A. McGeorge, 1919.

300 Yards: * G. A. McLaren, 1900; E. McLaren, 1916; A. McGeorge, 1919.

High Jump: * G. Watson, 1911; G. E. M. Govan, 1912; E. McLaren, 1916; A. McGeorge, 1919.

Broad Jump: G. Russell, 1915; E. McLaren, 1916; A. McGeorge, 1919.

Relay Race: 1919.

A. McGeorge in 1919 broke three records under 14 years, 100 yards, 11 4/5 secs.; 300 yards, 39 secs.; and Broad Jump, 16 ft. 1 in.

G. A. Smith in 1932 broke the record in the Mile (4 mins. 45 4/5 secs.).

G. E. M. Govan in 1916 tied with record in the High Jump (5 ft. 3 ins.).

The School Team won the Relay Race at the Infirmary Seven-a-Side Sports in the first three years, 1932-3-4, in which it was run.

SWIMMING

1909. N. Riches: East of Scotland Junior Championship.

1910. J. P. Gorman, N. Riches and W. Gerrard, East of Scotland and Scottish National Team Championships.

1919-20. J. P. Gorman, Swimming Blue, Oxford.

SHOOTING

In 1869 the Edinburgh and Midlothian Rifle Club offered a prize to be competed for by Edinburgh Schools. In 1870, seven Edinburgh Schools (Academy, Collegiate, Craigmount, Institution, Loretto, Merchiston, and R.H.S.) subscribed five guineas each to purchase the Trophy. It was won by the School in 1869, 1871-2, 1875-6-7-8, 1880, 1882. No reference is made in our records to any competition later than 1885.

* From 1900-11 the event was under 13.

ATHLETIC RECORDS

OFFICERS' TRAINING CORPS

In 1932 and 1933, at the East of Scotland Schools O.T.C. (Junior Division) Camp, Lance-Corporal Bugler Jay won the Silver Challenge Bugle. This is the first time this Bugle has been won two years running.

GOLF

Stewart H. Gordon: Championship of Transvaal, 1910.
Thomson, E. L.: Spiers Cup, 1929, 1930.
Scotland v. England (Boys' International), 1930.

BADMINTON

E. W. Wilson: England, 1932-3-4; Ireland, 1932-3-4.

ROWING

W. S. Kenneth; Junior Sculls, All-India Regatta, 1934.

SNOW-SHOEING

1891. A. N. Mouat: Steeplechase Championship, Winnipeg (record time).
1893. St. George's Club Championship.

SCHOOL SONG

SCHOLAE REGIAE EDINENSIS CARMEN

Words by Dr Marshall   *Music by A. C. Mackenzie*

VIVAS Schola Edinensis,
Schola Regia venerabilis!
Sicut arx in colle sita,
Sicut sol e nubibus densis,
Splendes, splendeas in aeternum,
Alma Mater atque amabilis:

Quo in aevo tu vetusto,
Inter parva infans parvula,
Faustis tamen omnium votis
Domicilio in angusto
Cursum tuum ad honores
Iniisti, vaga, tremula—

Tum gavisa est Doctrina,
Gaudent Leges, gaudent Artes;
Mater enim tu bonorum
Surgis altera Erycina,
Inter Gratias atque Amores
Splendidas actura partes.

Vivas, atque in annos crescas,
Alma Mater, Schola amata!
Omnium particeps honorum
Surgas semper, neu compescas
Studium tuum gloriae sacrum;
Fausta sis, felix, beata!

ROYAL HIGH SCHOOL

Liberi tui te laudamus
Laeto omnium cum clamore,
Et quum multis posthac annis
Tui quam juvenes amabamus,
Senes rursus meminerimus,
Vi clamabimus haud minore.

Hac ex vita nos cesserimus,
Nomen nostrum mox peribit;
Sed in saecula mortis expers
Tu manebis et veterrimus
Honos tuus revirescens
Juniores anteibit.

Vivas Schola Regia!
Vivas Schola Regia!
Vivas, Vivas,
    Schola Regia!

CALENDAR

Medals, Prizes, Trophies, Scholarships and Bursaries are omitted, as a chronological list of these is given on pp. 110-124. Class Clubs are similarly recorded on p. 101. Names of Rectors are printed in capitals.

CALENDAR

CALENDAR

CALENDAR

RHS 1ᵉᵗ XV 1956-57

Pringle Fisher   James. Blake. Gavin Lockhart

Kenneth Campbell.

Kenneth Orr.

Joe Millan

Alf (BALL) Swinton Crichton.

Richard Wallace

Bryan Ronaldson.

A. David McAdam

George Farlowe.

Malcolm McSwan.

Campbell Robb

AND

William J. Swanston.

Alan J. Minto

Michael Russell

Andrew Hunter

James Anderson

Alan A. Coghill

Stuart McFarlane

Gordon Grahamslaw

Jn. Gordon Glenn

Alexander W.W. Thomson

Sandy Gilley

Frank McGuire

Kenneth Arthur

Robert Laurie

Peter J. Finlay

Harry Richardson.

Robert W Dodds

Robert S. Miller

Brian M. Palmer.

William G Chapman

N. A. Arthur

J. Ogilvie

Ronald Leuchars

Graham A Romanis

Ian A Gordon

Robert D. Dewar

Adrian S. Mackintosh.

Robert Mactaggart

Alan J. Mars

Norman Black.

Stuart W. R. Miller

Robert. Hutchison

Douglas C. Jeffrey

George A. McManus

J.H. Montgomery

Ian S. Brown

Robert M Purves.

Ian McTavish

B. M. Paul

C. R. Davidson.

Derek Stoffman

John McCool.

Douglas R. Brown

G.M.Smith

Alexander G. Scott

Malcolm Halley

Douglas Boyd.

James Christie.